Stories
to make you
think

Text copyright © Heather Butler 1999
Illustrations copyright © Simon Smith 1999

The author asserts the moral right to be identified
as the author of this work

Published by
The Bible Reading Fellowship
First Floor, Elsfield Hall
15–17 Elsfield Way, Oxford OX2 8FG
ISBN 1 84101 034 0

First edition 1999
10 9 8 7 6 5 4 3 2 1

Acknowledgments
Unless otherwise stated, scripture quotations are taken from the
Good News Bible published by The Bible Societies/HarperCollins
Publishers Ltd UK © American Bible Society, 1966, 1971, 1976, 1992

A catalogue record for this book is available
from the British Library

Printed and bound in Great Britiain
by Bookmarque Ltd, Croydon, Surrey

Stories
to make you
think

Heather Butler

Introduction

This book addresses a range of topical and often sensitive issues relevant to the lives of children aged 6–10. It can be used on a one-to-one basis with the individual child, in a group or with a whole class, particularly during Circle Time or PSE.

Each chapter follows the same format:

1. Introductory Bible text relevant to the story.
2. The story itself. Most of the stories are based on real-life incidents. Each one includes suggested questions to encourage discussion. These have been used with groups of children and some of their comments are included in the text. If you wish to shorten the story, the sentences written in italics can be omitted without disruption to the story line.
3. Other things children have said which are not included in the main text.
4. Pauses in the text to provide time for reflective thought.
5. Prayers for use in a Christian context.

Contents

*This book is dedicated to the
memory of Poppy.*

*With special thanks to all the children who
helped in the research and writing.*

Going
to a funeral

God sets the time for birth and the time for death…
he sets the time for sorrow and the time for joy, the
time for mourning and the time for dancing… the
time for silence and the time for talk.

Ecclesiastes 3:2–7

Just before his own death, Jesus said to his friends,
'Do not be worried or upset… believe in God and
believe also in me. There are many rooms in my
Father's house, and I am going to prepare a place for
you. I would not tell you this if it were not so.'

John 14:1–2

That 'place' is where we will be with God after our death. Christians believe this promise is for everybody who follows Jesus.

Sam had to go to his grandfather's funeral. Before he went he was not sure if he really wanted to go.

Saying 'goodbye' to Poppy

'I don't want to go,' Sam moaned.

'Well you've got to,' Mum said.

'Why can't I go to Tom's house instead?' Sam tried again.

'Because you are coming to your grandfather's funeral and that is that,' Mum replied. 'Now hurry up. You're not even dressed and we've got to go in ten minutes.'

Sam slouched upstairs and got out his football kit. He looked up to see Mum standing in the doorway of his bedroom.

'No,' she said, 'don't even think about it. Put on the new top I bought you yesterday. And don't forget to clean your teeth.'

Mum was stressed. Not just a little bit, but *really* stressed.

Why was Mum getting cross with Sam?

'...he wasn't getting ready and she wants to go...'

'...she doesn't want to be late...'

'...she's taking it out on him because she's upset...'

'...she's not really angry with him...'

'...but he can't answer her back or he'll get in worse trouble...'

'Postman's been,' Dad called out to no one in particular. 'Looks like another card.'

Sam heard the lid of the bin in the kitchen bang against the wall as the envelope was thrown away. He finished getting dressed and went to the bathroom. As he put his toothbrush back on the shelf he heard Mum having a go at his big brother. It sounded as if James had emptied everything in the bin all over the kitchen floor. Mum wanted to know what on earth he thought he was doing.

'Dad didn't tear the stamp off that envelope,' James said. 'Doesn't he know we're collecting stamps at school to get money for guide dogs?'

'Yes he does,' Mum sighed, 'but Dad's got other things to think about at the moment.'

After that there was silence.

Sam decided that today was going to be a bad day—like every day since last Saturday.

The phone had rung first thing in the morning. A few minutes later, Sam had wandered into the kitchen to get his breakfast. He had a bit of a shock because Dad was sitting at the table crying his eyes out. Mum told him Poppy had died.

Sam knew about dying because his pet gerbil had died last year. Mum had sat with him then while he had cried. She was doing the same now for Dad.

Sam was not sure what to do. Should he leave the room or should he stay?

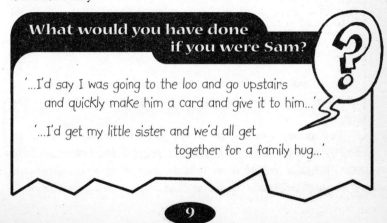

What would you have done if you were Sam?

'...I'd say I was going to the loo and go upstairs and quickly make him a card and give it to him...'

'...I'd get my little sister and we'd all get together for a family hug...'

> '...I'd go to my room and stay there until I heard them come out of the kitchen...'

In the end Sam simply went and stood by his mum and dad. Mum looked up and whispered, 'We'll come and find you when we're ready.'

'OK,' Sam whispered back.

He left them and found James, who was watching television. It was important to be with someone else. They had both loved their Poppy and now he was dead and they would never see him again.

Who would you want to be with if you had just been told that someone had died?

'...my pussy cat...'   '...my mum...'   '...my dad...'

'...my mum and dad, both of them...'

'...my baby brother...'   '...my guinea pig...'

'...myself. I'd want to be on my own...'

'...the dead person's body...'

Later that morning, Dad left to drive down to Nanny's. Sam went to play on the computer. Deep inside, he wanted to pretend Poppy was still alive.

When Dad came home that evening he was very tired. He and Mum went into the front room together and closed the door.

'They want to talk without us,' James whispered. 'Let's go upstairs and get ready for bed.' It seemed important to help Mum and Dad and that seemed the best thing to do. Sam was just dropping off to sleep when Dad came into his bedroom.

Sam opened his eyes and put his arms out for a hug.

'Poppy's not in pain any more,' Dad said, kneeling down beside the bed.

'I know,' Sam said. Then he asked, 'Is his body still in his bed where he died?'

'No, the funeral directors have taken it away.'

'Who?' Sam said. He had never heard of a 'funeral director' before.

'They're the people who look after the body and organize the funeral,' Dad said.

'Oh. Dad, can you video the football for me tonight?'

Even as he said it, Sam wondered if he had said the right thing. Mum had told him and James they were to be gentle with

Dad. Was asking him to video football being gentle?

Sam need not have worried.

'You are wonderful,' Dad said as he gave him another hug. 'You and James have got a special job to do this week,' he added.

'What's that?' Sam asked.

'Just be yourselves,' Dad said and kissed the top of Sam's forehead.

He stood up.

'Don't forget the football,' Sam called out as he walked towards the door.

'I won't,' Dad promised.

And now it was five days later and they were in the car, driving to the funeral.

'What will happen at the service?' James asked as they reached the bottom of their road.

Sam thought it was going to be very boring.

'We'll be in church,' Mum said. 'People will cry and get upset.'

'I'm not going to cry,' James interrupted. 'It's sissy to cry.'

'There's nothing wrong in crying,' Dad said, 'and it will be sad because we're saying "goodbye" to Poppy and giving thanks to God for his life.'

'Who'll be there?' James asked.

'All sorts of people. From where Poppy used to work and the bowls club, and there will be some relatives you've never seen.'

James sighed.

'At least they can't say how much we've grown if they've never seen us before,' he said.

He got fed up with grown-ups telling him how tall he was. Children were supposed to grow, so why did adults say silly things about it when they did?

'Where will Poppy's body be?' Sam asked, noisily turning over a page of the football magazine he was trying to read.

Mum sighed. She had been through this, and what would happen at the service, with both the boys already, so that they would know what was going on.

'His coffin with his body in will be at the front of the church,' she said.

Sam wrinkled up his nose. There had been a coffin on a television programme he had watched yesterday. A ghost had jumped out of it and scared people. He needed to make sure that was not going to happen today.

Mum seemed to have read his thoughts.

'The coffin will be closed,' she added, 'so you won't see Poppy's body.'

'And he won't become a ghost and jump out and say "hello" to us, will he?' Sam asked.

'No,' Mum replied.

'Dad saw Poppy's dead body last Saturday, didn't he?' James said.

Sam gave up trying to read his comic and put it down on the seat next to him.

'What did it look like?' he asked.

'As if Poppy was asleep,' Dad said. 'They'd dressed him in his favourite suit.'

'Wasn't it creepy?' Sam wanted to know.

'No,' Dad said. 'Just very peaceful.'

They were quiet for a few seconds, then Sam asked Mum and Dad, 'You're not going to die, are you?'

'Well, I will one day,' Dad replied, 'but not for a long time yet, I hope.'

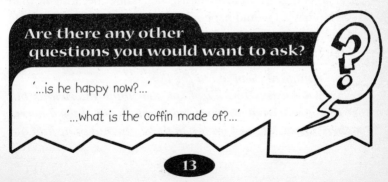

Are there any other questions you would want to ask?

'...is he happy now?...'

'...what is the coffin made of?...'

13

Sam tried to count how many white cars there were on the other side of the motorway. He had just reached twenty-two when Mum asked what they remembered most about Poppy.

'Playing chess and going to the park with him,' James said straight away.

'Seeing him wrapped up in a blanket and showing him my new game,' Sam added, thinking of the last time that he had seen him.

'Is that a nice memory?' Mum asked.

Sam nodded.

It was like Poppy.

He had been nice to be with even though he had sometimes told them off, like when he and James had walked all over the carpet in their muddy shoes.

'You know that after the service everyone will go to the hall along the road for something to eat and drink,' Mum said.

Sam sat up.

He had not been told that before. Maybe the bit in church would not be too bad if there was food at the end of it. And after the food they would be going to the crematorium for another little service and Poppy's coffin would be left there. Later on it would be burnt and the ashes buried in the ground. That was what happened at crematoriums. Sam knew because he had asked Mum what would happen to the body after the service. He also knew that some people's coffins are buried in the ground without being burnt.

Dad reminded them about the flowers.

'Everyone wants to talk about something afterwards but they're not sure what,' he said, 'so they talk about the flowers.'

There would be some on top of the coffin and some laid out

14

at the crematorium. They had got to look out for the yellow and blue ones because they were from him and Mum and James and Sam. Dad had ordered that colour because those were the same colours as Poppy's football team.

Eventually they arrived at Nanny's. James and Sam went upstairs to keep out of the way. Quite a few people were coming and going to and from the house.

James was watching out of the window while Sam read his football magazine.

'Dad's wearing a suit,' James suddenly whispered and began giggling. Sam went over to have a look. Dad did not very often wear a suit. He looked a bit funny in it.

'Bet Mum's in that black dress she bought yesterday,' James said. 'She put it in the boot this morning.'

It was not long before Mum came upstairs for the boys. She was now wearing… her black dress.

'Told you,' James whispered to Sam as they tiptoed downstairs behind her.

The hearse, with Poppy's coffin in it, had drawn up outside Nanny's house. People got into their own cars and followed as it drove, very slowly, to the church. When they arrived, four men lifted the coffin on to their shoulders. The vicar, who was going to take the service, came out to meet them.

'Where are the people from the bowls club?' Sam asked Mum as they walked up the church path.

'Inside the church already,' she whispered back. 'Only the family come in behind the coffin.'

By now they had reached the church. There was a brief pause, then the vicar started saying something in a loud voice and led the funeral procession into the building.

Sam was surprised at how light and warm the church was. Churches on television programmes were sometimes dark and spooky, but not this one.

A man in a black suit gave him a printed sheet of paper.

'Thank you,' Sam whispered.

The man gave him a little smile.

Sam did not look at the sheet of paper until he was sitting down next to Mum at the front of the church. It had Poppy's full name written at the top.

'I'm never going to see Poppy again,' Sam thought and suddenly felt very small. He hadn't really believed Poppy was dead until that moment, sitting there in this great big building with the coffin in front of him.

As the tears rolled down his cheeks, he buried his face in Mum's dress. It was safe there with her arm round him. The vicar was saying that a funeral was like opening a letter. If you thought of Poppy's body as the envelope, it was what was *inside* that was the important bit. Today they were going to think about the letter God had just received. They were going to think about Poppy and, in doing so, say 'goodbye' to him.

Sam wondered if God had a flip-top bin with a lid that banged on the wall if you flicked it too hard, and did he put the bodies in there when they arrived. He decided God probably did not. Anyway, if he did have a bin with a flip-top lid, it would work perfectly and not bang against the wall.

The service lasted for about half an hour. There were readings and prayers and the vicar reminded them of some of the things Poppy had done when he was alive.

After that first great wave of sadness Sam was all right. He did not actually enjoy the funeral, but it was not too awful and he knew that everyone around him was feeling the same as him. In a funny sort of way he found that a nice thought.

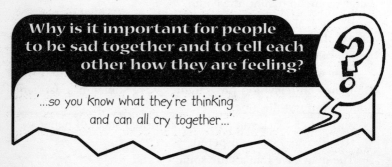

Why is it important for people to be sad together and to tell each other how they are feeling?

'...so you know what they're thinking and can all cry together...'

'...because you need to...'

'...grown-ups don't always think
children feel things but we do...'

When the service was over they all followed the coffin out of church and waited while it was put back in the hearse to be taken to the crematorium.

No one spoke much as they walked along the road to the hall. Once they got inside the hall the adults did not seem to be hungry. James and Sam did not mind because it meant they could get at the food first. They piled their plates as high as they dared and retreated into a corner to start eating.

They were the only children there. All their cousins were older and sat with the grown-ups.

After a while, Mum suggested the two of them went outside. That sounded like a good idea. They were getting tired of being quiet and good all the time. There was a park nearby and Mum said that they could let off steam across there if they were very careful crossing the road and did not get too much mud on their clothes.

They had only been in the park for ten minutes when James announced that he was still hungry. 'And it's boring here,' he added.

Sam agreed with him on both counts. He had hoped for something better than two swings and a seesaw that did not work properly.

'Shall we go back and see if there's any food left?' he suggested.

James nodded.

When they went back inside the hall the first thing they noticed was the noise. People were chatting. There was even some laughter. Dad had taken his suit jacket off. Mum was digging into a sausage roll.

'Mum, why are people laughing?' Sam whispered. 'Aren't they sad about Poppy any more?'

Mum put her arm round him.

'We're all still sad,' she said, 'but everyone's starting to relax now.'

'Can we get some more food then?' Sam asked.

'You and your tummy!' Mum sighed, then she added, 'You two are wonderful. You've really kept Dad and me going these last few days just because you've been yourselves. We'll still get sad, as you will, about Poppy, but we've brought a lot of our sadness out in the open today and that's important.'

'Can I get some more food then?' Sam asked again, pulling away from her.

Mum handed him her plate.

'Can you get me another sausage roll as well?' she added.

'All right,' Sam said and gave her a little grin.

Other things children have said

'...I wanted to go in the attic in my nanny's house because my grandad used to go up there. But I wasn't allowed to. I really miss him...'

'...when my grandma was alive we always went to her house on a Tuesday. We always went to the park. I used to like going there because she loved me...'

'...before my grandad died it was really good because we always went on outings and had treats. I wish he was still alive...'

'...after my granny died I thought she was watching me...'

Think about someone who has died.
It could be someone famous or
someone you actually knew.

❂ What do you remember about them?

❂ Do you miss them a lot or a little?

❂ Why?

❂ What did you use to do with them?

❂ If you were to write them a letter,

what would you tell them?

Prayers

Dear God, thank you for .... and all
the good times we shared together. Amen

Dear God, at the moment I'm hurting and aching
inside because .... has died. I need to find a safe place
to cry and tell someone about it. Where shall I go? Amen

Dear God, I'm not looking forward to tomorrow because of the
funeral. Help me to say 'goodbye' to .... properly. Amen

Dear God, ... is very sad at the moment.
He/she is hurting inside because .... has died.
I'm really sad as well. Keep reminding us that you're here,
even if sometimes we do not understand why something has
happened and you seem to be a long way away. Amen

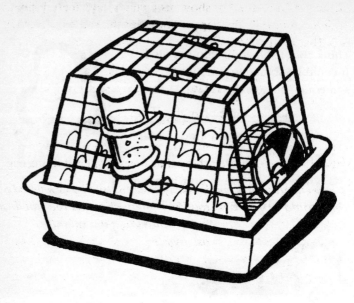

The death
of a pet

Mary arrived where Jesus was, and as soon as she saw
him, she fell at his feet. 'Lord,' she said, 'if you had
been here, my brother would not have died!' Jesus
saw her weeping... his heart was touched, and he was
deeply moved... Jesus wept.

John 11:32–35

Jesus was not afraid to show his feelings, and shared them with others—not only the happy times, but the sad ones as well.

That is what Toby did when his hamster died.

I'm going to miss you, my little friend

Fidget was Toby's hamster. He was very sweet, very loved and always listened to everything that was whispered in his ear.

Every Saturday, well, nearly every Saturday (somebody else had to do it if he was too busy) Toby changed the sawdust in Fidget's cage and cleaned out his little plastic house.

Each night, well, most nights (somebody else had to do it when he forgot, which was quite often) Toby would make sure Fidget had enough food and water for the next day. He would open the cage door and hold out his hand, and Fidget would run on to it. Then Fidget would climb all over Toby's back and shoulders and arms as he was taken downstairs to run around and be fed little bits of carrot or grape.

Fidget was just part of the family.

One day Toby bought him a little wooden tube to climb in and out of. But Fidget never really used it. In fact, as Toby said to Mum a few days later, he hardly ever came out of his house these days.

'How long do hamsters live for?' Toby asked.

'About two years,' Mum answered.

'How long have I had Fidget?' he whispered, though he knew the answer already.

'About two years,' Mum said.

She did not say anything else. Neither did Toby.

It was a Sunday when Dad suggested checking Fidget's cage. There had been no sound at all from him since last night and Dad was a bit worried.

Toby and Dad went upstairs.

Dad lifted Fidget's cage on to the floor.

No little whiskers twitched or wet nose poked out between the bars.

'He can't be dead,' Toby said in a brave sort of voice. 'I changed his water last night.'

'He hasn't touched it though, has he?' Dad said, as he gently lifted up the cottonwool bedding in the little plastic house.

Toby was glad Dad was there when he saw the cold, still ball of fur lying inside it. He put his head on Dad's lap.

'Why did Fidget have to die?' he sobbed.

Dad did not answer because there was nothing to be said. All living things have to die, but telling that to Toby at the moment would not help at all.

Instead, Dad whispered, 'It's all right to cry.'

He brushed away his own tears and stared at Fidget's little brown body, longing for it to move.

But it did not.

Fidget was gone.

For ever.

What do people do when they are upset?

'...I had a hamster but the next day she was dead. I cried...'

'...I got cross and my little brother came and I shouted at him to go away...'

'...some people try and be brave but they cry when they get home...'

'...we made a grave when our rabbit died.
I cried all the time for ages...'

*Dad stayed with Toby until he stopped crying.
'There are few animals who were so loved,' Dad
whispered. 'He was a very lucky hamster to have you
to look after him.'*

But not any more, Toby thought.

Eventually they put the cage, with Fidget still in it, back on the shelf where he had lived for the past two years.

'When you're ready,' Dad said, 'we'll bury him. But he can stay here for now.'

Several times during that day, Toby checked Fidget's cage. He wanted to make sure he was still there. He asked Dad if it was all right to pick up the little hamster even though he was dead. Dad said he could as long as he washed his hands afterwards.

Somehow the rest of the day passed. Whenever Toby tried to think of something else, he couldn't. His chest felt tight as well and his tummy had a funny sort of ache inside it.

He did not sleep very well that night and when he woke up, the first thing he did was peer inside Fidget's cage.

But Fidget did not come out and say 'hello' like he used to.

Toby got dressed and wandered downstairs. He was not looking forward to going to school, even though Mum had written a note telling his teacher about Fidget.

'Lots of your friends have had hamsters and other pets that have died,' she said, 'so they'll know how you're feeling.'

'I'm not going to cry though,' Toby said. 'It's not cool to cry.'

'It might not be cool,' Mum commented, 'but it's sensible.' Then she added, 'If you need me, ask your teacher to phone and I'll come and get you, OK?'

Toby nodded and ran his hand over the photograph of Fidget he had put in his pocket. He wanted to have it with him to remind himself of what Fidget had looked like.

Mum smiled at him.

It was a sad sort of smile.

She was tired because she had woken several times in the night waiting to hear the noise Fidget used to make when he was snuffling round his cage.

All she had heard was silence.

She decided to cook Toby his favourite pizza for tea to try and cheer him up, so during her lunch break she went to the supermarket. She had to fight back the tears when she passed the vegetables and the grapes.

I won't need to get Fidget's special treats any more, she thought and a wave of sadness swept over her.

She told Toby about it when he got home from school.

It helped him to know that someone else was finding it hard

as well. Then he told her how his friends had looked after him at school and told him all about when their pets had died and what they had done and how they had felt.

And life did not stop just because a hamster had died, and although he was still upset the pain did begin to get less as the days went by.

On Tuesday night, as Toby got ready for bed, he looked at Fidget for the last time. The following morning he asked Dad to take the cage downstairs.

'Do you want to bury him in the garden?' Dad asked.

'Not yet,' Toby whispered.

'That's fine,' Dad said. 'We'll leave him in the shed until you're ready.'

'OK,' he whispered.

It would not be long now before he was ready to say his final 'goodbye'.

Toby knew that and so did Dad.

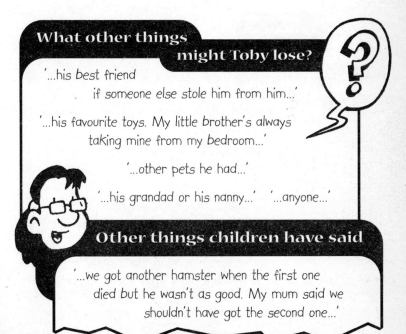

What other things might Toby lose?

'...his best friend
    if someone else stole him from him...'

'...his favourite toys. My little brother's always taking mine from my bedroom...'

'...other pets he had...'

'...his grandad or his nanny...'   '...anyone...'

Other things children have said

'...we got another hamster when the first one died but he wasn't as good. My mum said we shouldn't have got the second one...'

'...we stuck the goldfish down the loo. I wouldn't go for ages
in case it came back up and bit my bottom...'

'...we dressed up and did a proper service for my cat.
She was called Snowy. My Dad made a cross
and we stuck it on top of her in the ground...'

Thinking time

Think about your pets
and what they mean to you.

☺ If one of your pets has died,
what do you miss most about them?

☺ If they were here with you now,
what would you want to say to them?

Prayers

Dear God, you know what I'm feeling
like at the moment and how much I'm hurting
inside. Help me get through the next few days and
months until the pain starts to go away. Amen

Dear God, thank you for the people who look
after me while I say 'goodbye' to my pet. Amen

Dear God, thank you for ....
Thank you that she/he was so special. Amen

Dear God, thank you for all our pets and the love they
give us. Help us always to look after them properly. Amen

Families
are special

If a family divides itself into groups which fight
each other, that family will fall apart.

Mark 3:25

When Jesus said this, he was talking about what happens when people argue with each other. What do you think he meant when he used the word 'fighting'? Did he mean 'kicking and punching'?

1 Timothy 5:8 says that if we do not take care of our own families, we are not following the Christian faith. How can each of us look after our own family?

On Saturday mornings, Mum takes Jamie and Tom to the swimming-baths. She tries to make it a special time for them all.

Saturday morning

Jamie and Tom were twins. They lived with their mum, their dad, their pet rabbit called Herbert and their little sister, Annie.

Herbert lived in the garden, but was allowed to come into the house if the boys were with him and if he did not chew the sofa. Annie lived in the house with them and was allowed out most of the time, apart from when she was asleep. They thought she was a pain in the neck when she got into their toys and games, but 'OK' and even 'more than OK' the rest of the time.

So life was not too bad.

One of their favourite things was football training on a Tuesday evening. Dad came home early from work especially to take them. The three of them often went for a burger and chips afterwards as well. They liked that.

Their other favourite thing was on Saturday morning when Dad always looked after Annie. It was *his* time with her on his own. Today they were going to do some gardening together. That meant Dad would make himself a cup of coffee and read the paper while Annie pulled up some flowers and charged round the grass on her three-wheeler bike.

Then Dad would get out the lawnmower and Annie would cry, because she did not like the noise it made. So Dad would stop gardening until the others came home.

Mum knew this would happen. Tom and Jamie knew it

would happen too. They laughed about it in the car. But it did not matter. Life with a very little person around was like that sometimes.

Mum often had to work late on week-days, so on Saturday mornings she was all ears to find out what the twins had been up to during the week. She wanted to know what had happened at school, how their friends were, who they had played football with, which television programmes they been watching and anything else they wanted to tell her.

What sort of things would you talk about?

'...football...'

'...I'd ask her about what she was going to get me for my birthday...'

'...all the things I'd done at school...'

'...I'd want to tell her about whether my friends had been horrible to me or not...'

Mum would tell them about what she had been up to that week as well.

If Dad had got shopping to do, he and Annie sometimes had a lift into town with Mum and the boys. Occasionally he joined them in the swimming-pool and, after their swim, Annie would make a fuss because she would be taken into the girls' changing-room with Mum while Tom and Jamie went into the boys' with Dad.

Today, as they drove past the cinema, Jamie looked at the posters advertising which films were being shown. He fancied seeing one of them but it was useless telling Mum because she did not like going to the cinema. He would have to wait until they got home, and tell Dad.

Is there anything special you do with just one member of your family?

'...play level nine on the computer game with my dad...'

'...I like going to the Indian place for a meal with my mum...'

'...drawing pictures with my brother...'

'...playing football with my dad...'

'...going fishing with the grey-haired guy who's my dad...'

'...playing pool with my cousin...'

'...going up to town with my nan...'

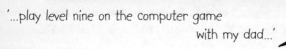

Mum parked the car outside the swimming-pool and went to get a ticket from the machine.

'There's just time to go to the shop,' she said, glancing at her watch.

She bought herself a magazine and the boys chose a comic and a packet of sweets each. She always treated them exactly the same. She would make a point of telling them she did.

Is there ever a time when one person in your family gets given more than you?

'...when our new baby came...'

'...if your brother's ill he might get more than you to help him get better...'

'...when it's your birthday...'

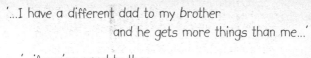

'...I have a different dad to my brother and he gets more things than me...'

'...if you're naughty then the others get a treat and you don't...'

'...if there's a baby brother like mine. He screams and Mum always goes to see what he's doing even if she's with me. It's all right sometimes for her to do that but not always...'

By ten o'clock, both boys were about to start their swimming lesson and Mum was sitting on a bench watching them—and reading her magazine at the same time. She knew she had got half an hour to herself before she joined them in the water for a swim in the main pool. That was her exercise for the week.

Tom was really pleased today. Not only had he learned how to do a racing dive, but he had also beaten Mum in a race to swim twice up and down the pool.

'You're getting good,' she gasped as she tried to get her breath back.

Tom splashed her and swam off. He was extra pleased because he'd beaten Jamie as well. Jamie had beaten him last week.

'Mum, have we got to go shopping?' Tom asked as they got out of the pool three-quarters of an hour later. Sometimes they went to the supermarket on the way home. That was really boring.

Mum shook her head.

'I managed to get it all done last night,' she said.

'Good,' Tom grinned. He wanted to read his comic and eat his sweets, not push a trolley and help decide which packets of cereal they would eat next week.

'Shall we go home, then?' Mum asked.

The boys nodded.

They liked Saturdays.

What things might have spoiled Saturday mornings for Mum or the boys?

'...if they had argued or been silly...'

'...if one of them had felt sick or been ill...'

'...if Mum had met one of her friends and stopped to talk to them for hours and hours. My mum does that and I get really bored. Then she tells me off—but it's her fault I got bored...'

'...if the boys had done something to embarrass their mum...'

'...Mums get stressed before they even start taking the kids out and we have to put up with them getting cross with us when it's not our fault...'

'...I don't like my mum and dad watching me all the time. I like to be more grown up and go places without her...'

'...the worst thing is when you have to behave yourself all the time if they take you some place you don't want to go to. That's dead boring...'

Thinking time

Think about the people who are in your family.

❂ What do you like doing most with them?

❂ Do you ever spoil family times?

❂ Does anyone else in your family spoil them?

❂ Is there anything you can do to make family times better?

Prayers

Dear God, thank you for our families and the fun we have together. Thank you for the love we show each other. Help us to make family times really special. Amen

Dear God, sometimes we fall out with each other and say nasty things. Help us not to, even when someone really annoys us. Amen

Dear God, you have put us in families so we can learn all sorts of things together. Please be with us as we grow up and help us get on with each other. Amen

A parent remarries

Children, it is your Christian duty to obey your parents, for this is the right thing to do. 'Respect your father and mother' is the first commandment that has a promise added: 'so that all may go well with you, and you may live a long time in the land'. Parents, do not treat your children in such a way as to make them angry. Instead, bring them up with Christian discipline and instruction.

Ephesians 6:1–4

In this passage, the apostle Paul says that children should respect their parents and do what they want them to do. In return, parents should not do things to make their children angry. Parents and children have to work together.

Joey's dad had left him and his mum. After a while, Joey's mum wanted to get married to someone else. Joey found that very hard. He had got used to having his mum all to himself. Neither did he like Uncle Dave's two children.

Do we have to live with them?

Joey sat very still and looked at the posters on his bedroom wall. He was trying to take in what Mum had just told him... that she and Uncle Dave were going to get married and, when they did, he and she would go and live in Uncle Dave's house with Uncle Dave's horrible children. Mum had not called them horrible but Joey thought they were.

A lot had happened over the last few years. First of all there had been Dad walking out after he and Mum had had the most enormous row. Joey had run up to his bedroom and buried his head under his quilt cover that day.

He could still remember it.

What do you do when grown-ups get cross with each other?

'...run out of the door and go and play outside...'

'...shout "stop it" at them...'

'...I wish I was brave enough to shout "stop it" at them but I'm not. My big sister wouldn't do it either...'

'...run upstairs and put really loud music on so I can't hear them...'

'...I always hide underneath my quilt and hold my teddy bear very tight. I hate it when they shout. Sometimes he throws something at her and she screams at him...'

'...they don't shout at each other when we're around but sometimes they don't speak to each other and you know they've had a row and they think we don't know but we do because you can tell from the way they look at each other...'

Joey had hardly seen his dad since then. They had been to the park and the burger bar and the cinema several times. Joey had enjoyed that. He had asked Dad once if he was ever coming back home. His dad had said no way, if his mum was still there.

Then Joey's dad stopped coming to see him. Mum said he had gone to live a long way away. Joey had never stayed at Dad's new flat or gone on holiday with him or been go-karting or done any of the other things he had been told they would do together.

At first Joey really missed his dad, but gradually he and Mum learned to live on their own. Mum got a job at the supermarket and said she could manage quite well by herself, thank you very much. She no longer needed his dad.

And then Uncle Dave turned up. Mum had met him at work. Joey liked him all right and it was nice to have someone to kick a football around with in the garden. They would go to the video shop together and have a laugh. Uncle Dave always bought him a huge packet of sweets from the corner shop when he came visiting. He had even given him a new bike for his birthday. At the time, Joey had wished it had been his real dad who had bought him his bike, and not Uncle Dave. But he had never told anyone that.

And then today had happened and he and Mum would soon

be living with Uncle Dave *and* his little boy *and* his little girl. That was the worst bit.

What would you be feeling if you were Joey?

'...sad and angry...'

'...Joey should have *been* asked
                if he wanted to live with them...'

'...he might think Uncle Dave wouldn't love him
                    as much as his own mum loved him...'

'...he wouldn't like it. He'd cry and be lonely and his mum
            would have to come upstairs and look after him...'

'I don't want to live with them,' was the first thing Joey said.

'Why not?' Mum asked.

'Because they play with my toys and break them,' he said.

'Not all the time, surely,' Mum sighed.

They do, Joey thought, remembering his Lego castle which little Adam had pulled apart last time he had been there.

'But Uncle Dave loves me,' Mum said. 'And you,' she added. 'He thinks the world of you.'

'He's all right, but not *them*,' Joey blurted out. 'Why do *they* have to come?'

He had got used to having Mum to himself, then sharing her a bit with Uncle Dave, but now he would have to have Selina and Adam as well. And he did not want that.

Ever.

Mum sighed and kissed the top of his head.

'They're all right, you know. I spent yesterday evening with them,' she said. 'When Chris was looking after you.'

Joey pulled away from her. He had been hurting before but suddenly he hurt even more.

'Do they know about you and Uncle Dave?' he asked. 'Did you tell them before me?'

Mum looked down at her watch.

'We told them last night,' she said. 'They were really excited about it—and so will you be when you've had time to get used to the idea. It's going to be lovely for all of us. Now, we're off to the cinema in five minutes so we'd better get ready.'

Mum had let him down like she had never ever let him down before. She had even told Selina and Adam about her and Uncle Dave before she had told him. Did she already love them more than him?

He suddenly hated her and his real dad. Why couldn't they have stayed together? Then this would never have happened!

Uncle Dave's house had three bedrooms. Which one would he have? Would he be allowed to put his football posters up? What would happen if Adam or Selina broke any of his toys? Would he tell Mum or would he tell Uncle Dave? Would Uncle Dave be nicer to them than he would be to him? Would Mum be nicer to them? What would happen if he wanted to watch one television programme and they wanted to watch a different one? There were two of them and only one of him.

Only one.

He was going to be all on his own. And they'd expect him to be good and play with the little ones while Mum looked after everyone else except him.

Mum's voice came up the stairs.

'Are you ready?' she called out.

I don't want to go, Joey thought. I want to stay here. On my own.

Then he had another thought. Maybe if he tried extra hard to be good Mum would love *him* more than the others. At least he had her to himself this afternoon. Joey wanted to see the film about dinosaurs, though Mum had said it might be too scary.

Joey had just reached the top of the stairs when the front door bell rang.

Mum went to open the door.

'Dad says we're to start calling you Mum,' a little voice called out.

'Hello, Adam,' Mum said and bent down to kiss him. Then she leaned over and kissed Selina who was in Uncle Dave's arms.

Why are they here? Joey thought.

'Hi there,' Uncle Dave called out. 'Are you ready? We must get a move on, or we'll be late. Selina and Adam have wanted to see the new cartoon film for ages.'

'I thought it was just me and Mum going to the cinema,' Joey stammered. 'I wanted to see the dinosaur film.'

'I know, darling,' Mum said, 'but that wouldn't be suitable for Selina and Adam and we're going to the cinema this afternoon to be one big happy family and sit together.'

'But...' was all Joey could say. 'What about me? Don't I count any more?'

What would you have done if you were Joey?

'...I'd have gone, and done everything Mum wanted so that she would have loved me more than the others...'

'...I'd leg it back upstairs as fast as I could and shut the door...'

'...I'd have asked for a lollipop or something like that and made sure the others didn't have one just to show them...'

Uncle Dave winked at Mum. 'Don't worry,' he said, 'I'd like to see the dinosaur film, too. Perhaps I could take Joey and his friends to see that later on...'

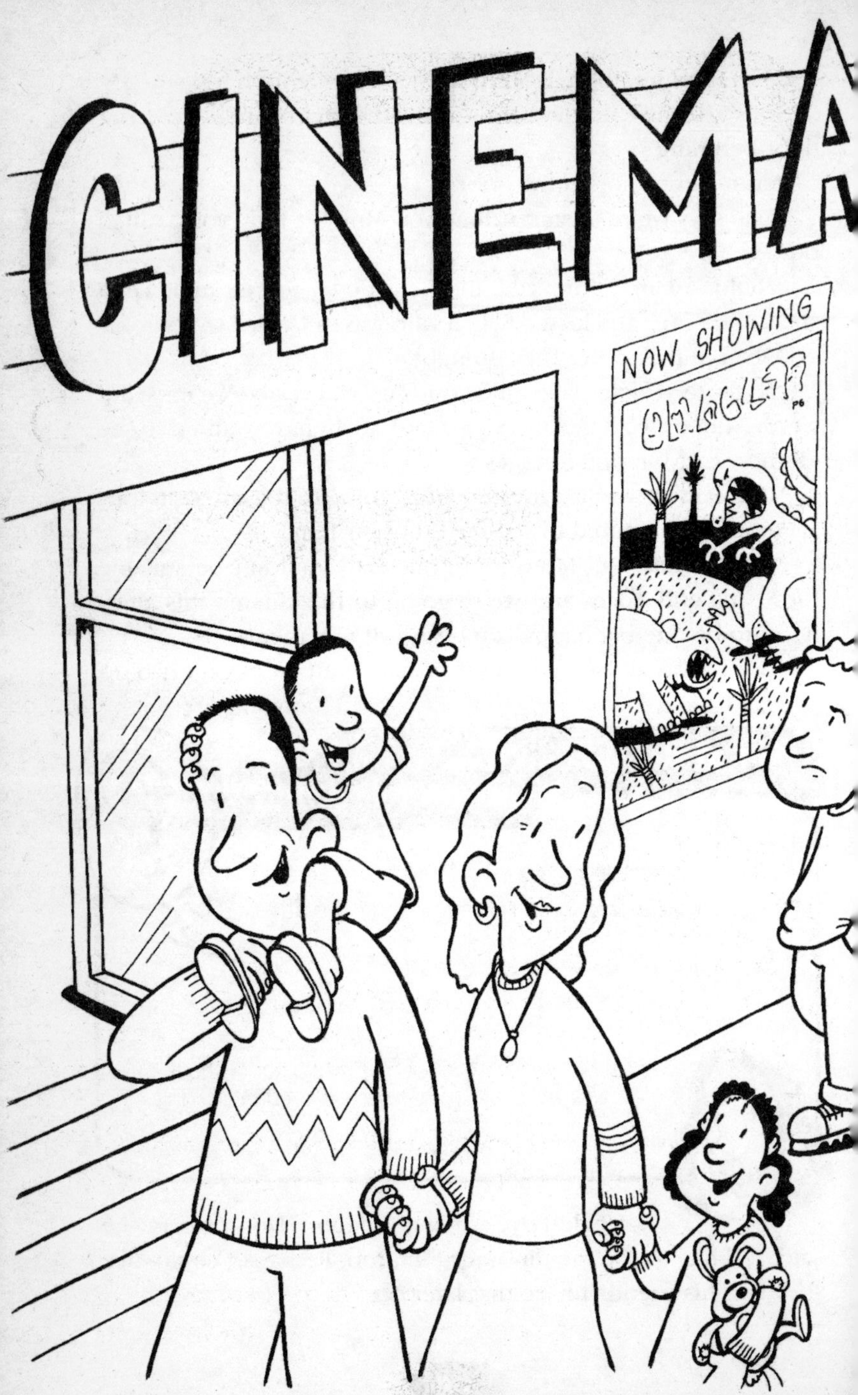
CINEMA
NOW SHOWING

'...I was about two years old and my mum *broke* up with my dad. I am eight now and I only ever see him on Sundays. My mum and me and my brother were homeless for ages. My mum's getting married again next month and I'm going to be bridesmaid...'

'...Children should be told what their mums and dads are doing. Moving in with other children is horrible. I like them now, though...'

Thinking time

Think about one person in your family.

- ✪ What do you think about them?
- ✪ What do they think about you?
- ✪ If you think they don't like you, what can you do to help them get on better with you?
- ✪ If you think they *do* like you, how do you know?

Prayers

Dear God, sometimes things happen that we don't like and cannot change. Thank you that you have promised always to be with us and love us whatever happens. Amen

Dear God, sometimes it's hard to like other people but I have to try and be nice to them. Please help me. Amen

Dear God, I don't like what's happening to me at the moment. Help me to get through tomorrow. And the next day. And the one after that. Amen

Moving
to a new town

The Lord said to Abram, 'Leave your country,
your relatives, and your father's home, and go to a
land that I am going to show you. I will give you many
descendants, and they will become a great nation.
I will bless you and make your name famous,
so that you will be a blessing.'

Genesis 12:1–2

Moving away from the home you've lived in for a long time is never easy. The Bible has many stories about people who moved: Joseph went to Egypt and later became a ruler of the country, Paul travelled to new places and always found friends to look after him. For Abram the move away from his home led to many adventures which he might never have experienced if he had not done as God had asked. We need to remember that even if everything else changes, God does not, and he will always be with us, wherever we are.

In Ecclesiastes 3:2, the writer talks about a 'time for planting' and a 'time for pulling up'. When you move it's like 'pulling yourself up' and then 'planting yourself' in a new place.

Navdeep's family were moving and she did not want to go.

The day before moving day

The idea of moving had all happened rather quickly. First of all, Dad had been offered a new job. Then he and Mum had gone away for a weekend while Navdeep stayed at Julie's. When they came back she was told they had bought a new house where she would have a bigger bedroom to sleep in and a bigger garden to play in. They would be moving in three months' time.

Navdeep was supposed to be excited about it.

Only she wasn't. The nearer the time came to moving day, the less excited she felt. She was dreading it. Finally the day arrived when there was only one day left. Tomorrow the removal men would be arriving to load everything up into their great big van.

Navdeep slopped some milk on to the table. She had been aiming for her cereal bowl and missed. Mum told her to clean it up.

'Not with a tea towel,' Mum said in an irritated sort of way. 'Get a cloth.'

'I don't want to move,' Navdeep suddenly said as she wiped the table. 'I want to stay here with my friends but nobody ever asks me what *I* want to do.'

Mum sighed.

'Navdeep,' she said, 'we've been through this I don't know

how many times already. Dad has to move with his job, and if he doesn't work we can't buy clothes or food or go on holiday or have a house or anything like that. So just accept it, will you? We are moving and that is that.'

'And you *are* getting a bigger bedroom and a bigger garden to play in,' she added. 'Much bigger than I ever had when I was your age. And you'll soon make some new friends, you know that.'

Navdeep pulled a face. Not too much of a face in case Mum saw it and told her off again. Mum had told her off a lot lately.

What things might have been particularly worrying Navdeep?

'...making new friends...'

'...scared that the removal men might leave her favourite toys behind...'

'...everything is safe where she is and it won't be safe at her new school...'

'...she doesn't want to leave her teachers and friends...'

'....she doesn't know if her new teacher will like her...'

'...she might be lonely...'

'...her mum's cross with her...'

Navdeep finished her breakfast and got ready for school. This year her teacher's name was Mrs Grasswell and she was really, really nice. Today, as Navdeep and Julie walked into the classroom, a girl they had never seen before was standing by the teacher's chair.

Mrs Grasswell looked up and smiled at them both.

'Hello, you two,' she said. 'I've got a special job for you both.

This is Amy who's come all the way from America and is joining our class. Could you look after her today and show her what to do?'

Navdeep looked at Amy. She did not look very happy.
'Will that be all right, then?' Mrs Grasswell asked.
The girls nodded and started talking to Amy.

How would you help if Amy came to your school?

'...I'd show her what to do...'

'...I'd look after her...'

'...I'd let her come to my house...'

'...I'd help her get her work right...'

'...I'd let her join in our games...'

'...I'd tell her what the teacher and the dinner ladies are like...'

'...I'd tell her everyone's names...'

They did not have long before Mrs Grasswell asked everyone to sit on the carpet while she took the register. Amy sat down between Julie and Navdeep. She went bright red and whispered in a strong American accent, 'Yes, Mrs Grasswell' when her name was called out.

'Can I go to the bathroom?' she then asked.

Mrs Grasswell said she could go to the toilet and asked Julie to go with her. As the door closed behind them someone started giggling.

'What's the matter?' the teacher asked, staring at the boy who had giggled.

'That new girl talks funny,' he said.

'And I expect,' Mrs Grasswell said, 'that to Amy, *you* talk funny, too. But Amy's not giggling at you, is she? She's got more sense. Now I'll have no more of it. We've all got to help Amy because it must seem very strange coming here.'

Navdeep suddenly wondered if *she* would sound different to everyone else when she moved. She had not thought of that before. If she did, she hoped no one would laugh at *her*.

Julie and Navdeep rather enjoyed showing Amy round the school, telling her what they were allowed to do at playtime and going through the names of all the teachers.

'We're allowed on the climbing-frame on a Tuesday when it's Mrs Dawson's playground duty,' Julie said as they put their coats on at playtime.

Amy smiled.

'We didn't have a climbing-frame like this at my last school,' she said, 'but we did have a swimming-pool. We had one in our back garden as well.'

'If you get a sticker for doing good work,' Navdeep said, 'you have to go to Mrs Longford and she gives it to you.'

'Mrs Longford's the head teacher,' Julie added. 'She lives in the office with Mrs Jones the secretary. You have to take the register to her when it's your turn.'

'My old teacher used to give us a sticker if one of our teeth came out,' Amy said.

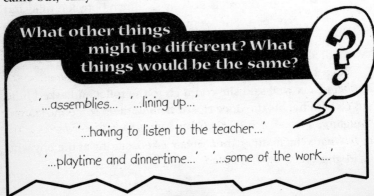

What other things might be different? What things would be the same?

'...assemblies...' '...lining up...'

'...having to listen to the teacher...'

'...playtime and dinnertime...' '...some of the work...'

'...all the people...'

'...the weather would be different
if you moved to a different country...'

'...what the classroom is like inside...'

'...the teacher...'

'You seem to be making new friends all right,' the dinner lady said to Amy as they filed into the dining-hall at lunchtime. She went to fetch an extra chair so Amy could squeeze on to the same table as Julie and Navdeep.

Then she turned to Navdeep.

'And you leave today, don't you?' she asked. 'So Amy can have *your* seat tomorrow.'

The dinner lady had not meant to be unkind, but Navdeep suddenly felt sad because Julie would have Amy as a new friend instead of her. She did not like that thought and tried to put it out of her mind as they sat down and opened their lunch boxes.

'I'm going to e-mail my best friend tonight,' Amy said as she took out an enormous sandwich. 'Her mum wants to know what this school is like.'

Navdeep looked at Julie. She could phone *her* best friend and talk to her, which would be even better. Navdeep decided that that was what she was going to do.

At home-time, Mrs Grasswell said 'goodbye' to Navdeep and gave her a present. It was a little book and everyone in the class had written their names on the front page. That was rather nice.

'Let's say a special prayer for Navdeep,' Mrs Grasswell said as she gave it to her.

'Dear God,' the teacher began, 'please be with Navdeep tomorrow as she moves. Keep her safe and help her make lots of friends in her new school. Amen'

'Amen,' everyone repeated.

'We're going into town tonight,' Amy said as they lined up to leave the classroom. 'Mum says we'll get a burger and chips because she hasn't unpacked all the cooking things yet.'

They collected their coats and bags from the cloakroom and walked out into the playground. A lady was standing just outside the door on her own. All the other mums were chatting by the school gate or milling round the playground.

'Had a good day?' the lady greeted Amy.

'Hi, Mom, it was great,' Amy said. 'That girl's called Julie and here's Navdeep and there's Janette and Paula and my teacher's called Mrs Grasswell and there's the dinner lady who looked after us at lunchtime. She's Pete's mum, and Charlotte's having a party next week.'

She paused for breath.

'OK, OK,' her mum said. 'And don't forget you've got to e-mail Sonia tonight. You'll have a lot to tell her.'

Amy nodded and jumped up and down.

Will *I* be like that? Navdeep wondered as she stood in the playground holding her PE bag and some books to take to the next school.

She hoped so.

Mum was talking to Mrs Longford. Navdeep walked across to where they were standing.

'I was just saying "goodbye" and "thank you",' Mum said.

'Well, Navdeep,' Mrs Longford smiled. 'The next few weeks will be full of new things, won't they? Remember, grown-ups are funny things. They don't always let children know what they're feeling inside. But that doesn't mean you don't have to tell them what *you're* feeling. If you're feeling sad, say something. Do you promise?'

Navdeep nodded and they got ready to go.

'Mum,' Navdeep said as they walked home. 'Do you *really* want to move?'

Mum paused before she answered. Then she said, 'Put it like this. I'll be glad when the next few weeks are over. I don't want to leave all my friends and our house and the things we know here. It's hard work packing up and I'm very tired at the moment. But it's quite exciting to think about all the new friends we'll be making and all the new places there'll be to explore.'

'We had a new girl in our class today,' Navdeep said. 'She's going to have a burger and chips tonight. Can we?'

Mum looked at her daughter and smiled.

'Good idea,' she said. 'I can't face cooking and there's nothing much in the fridge anyway. We could even go to the Pasta House if you'd prefer.'

Navdeep thought about it for a moment.

'Can we get a burger tonight and find a pasta place tomorrow?' she asked hopefully.

Would you enjoy having to move?

'...we moved and it was horrible. I cried all the way over here...'

'...I've never moved so I don't know what it's like...'

'...we had to when Mum left Dad. I'm glad now because I've got lots of friends and I prefer living here than where we used to live...'

'...my mum was dead stressed and shouted at us. She shouted at Dad as well...'

Other things children have said

'...You don't change just because you go to a different school, and you'll be scared so you won't do your best work. But you would be the same...'

'...she might think someone was going to steal her best friend from her as soon as she left...'

Thinking time

Think about a time when you had to go to a place you'd never been to before.

- Did you enjoy it?
- If so, why?
- If not, why not?
- Would everyone have felt the same as you did?
- How can you help other people?

Prayers

Dear God, thank you that you are everywhere and that you are always with us wherever we go. Amen

Dear God, I'm not looking forward to moving because

....

....

I think it's going to be really hard to make new friends. Please help me. Amen

Dear God, I'm excited about moving because

....

....

Thank you for my friends here and for the new ones I am soon going to make. Amen

Understanding more about God

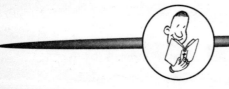

What we see now is like a dim image in a mirror; then we shall see face to face. What we know now is only partial; then it will be complete— as complete as God's knowledge of me.

1 Corinthians 13:12

Sing hymns of praise to the Lord; play music on the harp to our God. He spreads clouds over the sky; he provides rain for the earth and makes grass grow on the hills… He spreads snow like a blanket and scatters frost like dust.

Psalm 147:7–8 and 16

Lord, you have examined me and you know me.
You know everything I do; from far away you
understand all my thoughts. You see me, whether I am
working or resting; you know all my actions...
You are all round me on every side; you protect me
with your power... If I flew away beyond the east or
lived in the farthest place in the west, you would be
there to lead me, you would be there to help me.

Psalm 139:1–3, 5 and 9–10

In the busyness of life, it's not always easy to set time aside to think about God. Sometimes we need to give ourselves the space to stop and look around us; to think about our world and ourselves. In the Bible passages from 1 Corinthians and the Psalms, the writers have thought about the different aspects of our awareness of God: about heaven and creation, and the way he reaches into our innermost thoughts.

One day, when Mrs Simpson was taking her dog for a walk, she suddenly found herself thinking about God.

Waiting for Fred

It was a windy October morning and a watery sun had at last pulled itself into the sky. Mrs Simpson put on her coat and wellies and set off for the park. As usual, her dog, who went by the name of Fred, was at her side.

As soon as he was let off his lead, Fred disappeared and Mrs Simpson strolled along the path enjoying the fresh air and vibrant autumn colours all around her.

Every so often she called out Fred's name and listened for a snuffle or a grunting noise just to make sure he was still there, chasing rabbits he would never catch.

She found a tree stump and perched on the edge of it.

Today was so different from yesterday when it had rained and she and Fred had got soaking wet. She scrunched her boots into the leaves on the ground around her, loving the squelchy noise they made.

Mrs Simpson looked up. The clouds were scudding across the deep blue sky. The tops of the trees were swaying to and fro. This was the sort of day for flying kites and running across fields.

A day to feel free.

A day to enjoy being alive.

When is your favourite time of year? Why do you like it so much?

'...birthdays, because I get presents and stuff...'

'...Christmas because I like my roast dinner and pudding...'

'...spring because of the baby animals and growing loads of flowers...'

'...summer because Mum lets me go out every day and we have lots of holidays...'

'...winter because it snows and we make snowmen and it's nearly always deep...'

(No one liked autumn the best.)

Mrs Simpson's favourite time of year had *always* been autumn. As a child she had loved running through piles of dried leaves in the woods, kicking them up in the air and chasing them as they fell. She loved going home as well and curling up in the big chair by the fire in the front room.

Mrs Simpson suddenly remembered something else about when she had been a child, and smiled to herself. She must have been about seven and her teacher had used the word 'current' to describe the wind. Mrs Simpson had gone home and asked her mum why currants, as in the things you eat, were in the sky being blown around, and why couldn't she see them.

Mum had explained about curr*a*nts with an 'a' and curr*e*nts with an 'e' being two different things. One was a dried grape and the other, the one with the 'e', was when something was going by or through somewhere—like the wind or electricity or in the sea. You had to look at how it was spelt to know which was which. The currant with the 'a' was what you ate, the current with an 'e' was like electricity. Mrs Simpson had never got them confused again.

Ever.

That same teacher had talked about God. She had said that in some ways God was like the wind because you could not actually *see* him, you just knew where he was. Whenever you saw anything that was beautiful and lovely and good you knew that God was there, like a current running through that thing. It could be something in nature, or a person or animal. She had also said that you could choose whether or not you wanted to be swept up and blown along by God. You could choose to ignore him, because God doesn't force himself into your life— he wants you to invite him in.

Mrs Simpson knew what she thought about the wind but still was not sure what she thought about God.

What do you think about God?

'...he's like a cloud...'

'...he's like a big giant with a sports car...'

'...he thinks about us all the time...'

'...I don't think he exists at all...'

'...he's everything and he loves me...'

'...he's caring and gentle and nice and
like a dad that gets it right all the time...'

'...he's like fire and wind and rain. All those strong great big things. And he created the world as well. He's very clever...'

'...he wants us to be his friend...'

'...he's got a son called Jesus who was born at Christmas time and died at Easter. They put him on a cross but he came back to life again because he's dead strong...'

Someone Mrs Simpson knew talked about God as though he was a friend. This person said she talked to God—it was called praying—and said he answered her prayers, even though sometimes the answer was 'no' or 'not yet'. Mrs Simpson had often wondered what it would be like to talk to God like that. Maybe she should find out more about it. But for now she had to find that dog of hers. She'd been sitting and thinking for rather a long time and he'd probably got his nose stuck down a rabbit hole by now.

'Fred!' she yelled.

Silence.

'Fred!' she tried once more. 'I am going home and if you don't come with me there will be no biscuits for...'

Fred appeared. The word 'biscuit' usually worked.

'Good boy!' Mrs Simpson said, taking his lead out of her pocket. 'Have you had a nice time out there with the rabbits?'

Fred shook himself but said nothing.

Mrs Simpson laughed and, with Fred at her side, started for home. She thought of her big chair and bright fire. She looked up at the autumn sky.

'Thank you for Fred,' she said. 'Thank you for the fun we have together.'

At that moment Mrs Simpson felt Fred's scruffy tail brushing the top of her boots. And she smiled a secret smile.

Other things children have said

'...God's a ghost, like a spirit...'

'...he has hair all over his chest and face, like an old, old man...'

'...he's a big, thoughtful beam of light...'

'...he sent Jesus to die for us on a cross because he wanted us to be friends with him...'

'...he loves me...'

Thinking time

Think about whether or not you believe in God.

⊗ Is it important to believe in him?

⊗ Do you know anyone who does believe in him?

⊗ What have they said about him?

⊗ How could you get to know more about him?

Prayers

Dear God, there are lots of things we don't understand about you. Help us to understand more clearly. Amen

Dear God, thank you that you are everywhere and are always with us even though we sometimes forget about you. Amen

Dear God, help us to learn to trust you in all that we do, even when that is really difficult. Amen

Dear God, thank you for .... Amen

Valuing
ourselves

For God loved the world so much that he
gave his only Son, so that anyone who believes in
him may not die but have eternal life.

John 3:16

God does not love one person more than another. He loves each of us the same amount.

He does not have favourites.

To know you are loved and special just because you are you is very important. It took the wooden camel a long time to finally discover that.

The wooden camel

Helen and her mum went to the market. They ended up at a stall that sold carved wooden animals, and it was there that Helen first saw the little camel.

There was something very special about him.

'That's what I want to get for Simon and Lottie,' she said.

Mum looked where Helen was pointing, and a few minutes later the camel, and his cart, were lowered into Helen's waiting arms.

Helen had a good look at him.

'He's got such a sad face,' she said. 'Do you think I could make him smile?'

'I doubt it,' Mum said without really thinking.

Helen's hands stroked the smooth, hard hump of the camel's back.

'Anyway,' Mum said, 'we've got to wrap him up and send him to England tomorrow.'

Helen nodded.

At least she had the rest of that day to try and make him smile.

She called him Charlie. The camel rather liked that, though of course he couldn't tell her. He couldn't tell her, either, how proud he felt taking her little mouse for rides on his cart. Helen pulled him so gently and he loved the feel of her mouse's soft fur on his wood. She dressed him up in a blue ribbon and kept him close by her for the rest of the day. A little happy feeling had started to grow inside him for no other reason than because he knew he was loved.

'Charlie, smile for me,' Helen whispered.

But however hard he tried he could not move his mouth. He was made of wood and his face would never change.

How do people show you that you are loved?

'...they give you presents when you go to see them...'

'...they come and visit you...'

'...my mum gave my dad a card on Valentine's day last year and it was dead soppy...'

'...they could tell you...'

'...they listen to you when you want to tell them something...'

'...my mum gives me kisses...'

'Bye bye,' Helen whispered the following day. 'Thank you for letting me play with you and being my friend.' He did not know it but that was the last time he would ever hear Helen's voice.

Travelling halfway round the world covered in bubble-wrap, brown paper and string was not something the wooden camel enjoyed.

It was dark and he was hot and it was very uncomfortable being thrown about and dropped and having heavy things put on top of him, and there were strange, frightening noises that went on and on and on.

How many times did the wooden camel wish he was back with Helen? He lost count. All he knew was that the warm, happy feeling he had felt inside had disappeared.

At last the paper and bubble-wrap were ripped off and light burned into the back of his eyes. Someone was reading the card Helen's mum had put in the parcel.

'To Simon and Lottie. Hope you'll love this camel as much as Helen has done.'

The wooden camel found himself being put on a table in the middle of a room. And that was where he stayed. He had a new home, but it was not the same as Helen's.

He certainly never got bored here, for there was always something going on. Simon and Lottie raced in and out, going here, there and everywhere, usually followed by their mum or dad.

He had cars loaded on his cart. The wheels dug into his wood and hurt him. Or he'd be sold when the children played shops. He always seemed to be bought first and would find himself at the bottom of the shopping bag with other things shoved on top of him. When they were pretending to be doctors his front legs got bandaged up. It reminded him of the time Helen had gently wrapped a ribbon round his neck and he wished more than ever that he could have stayed with her.

He remembered how she had loved him and the warm happy feeling that he'd had inside him. All he felt now was empty and lonely and sad.

Have you ever felt really lonely?

'...when my friend goes off with someone else...'

'...if there's no one to play with in the playground...'

'...I have to go up to bed early when my mum has her friends round. I don't like that...'

Helen wanted me to smile, he thought, but how can you if no one ever tells you how much you're loved? The wooden camel looked across at Teddy who was sitting on the other end of the table dressed up in a tea towel and scarf. He was *definitely* loved. You could tell by the look on his face. It had a sort of smile on it all the time. Was it because he was soft and furry? The wooden camel could never be that.

Summer eventually gave way to autumn, which meant Simon's fifth birthday was about to happen.

One evening the children's mum sat down to write the invitations for Simon's birthday party. He was having a 'teddy bears' picnic' and seven of his friends were going to be invited.

You are invited to Simon's teddy bear birthday party on 3rd October at 4, Lynton Road at 2 o'clock.
Please bring your teddy bear with you.

It seemed an awfully long time before the party finally arrived. Simon got more and more excited about it. Eventually the 3rd of October arrived.

'If it doesn't rain we'll eat outside,' his mum said as she started to get things ready. 'There'll be less mess for me to clear up afterwards.'

By five past two, everyone was there. All the teddy bears were put on the table next to the wooden camel. The first game they were going to play was pass-the-parcel and they did not need them for that.

The next game was 'hunt-the-picture'. Dad had hidden fifty teddy bear pictures, which Mum had cut out of magazines, all over the house earlier in the day. Lottie found the most, partly because she had followed Dad round as he hid them, so she knew where they all were.

After that they watched a cartoon on the video—about teddy bears, of course.

'We'll risk the weather and go outside for our picnic,' Mum said as it finished.

At least I can see everyone through the window, the wooden camel thought as he watched little hands grabbing their teddies. Then someone picked *him* up as well and he found himself on the edge of a blanket outside with the other teddies and the children and the plates of chips and hot dogs and the cakes and crisps and chocolate biscuits and drinks that kept getting knocked over and…

He was part of the party. They wanted him here. Someone even tried to squirt tomato sauce all over him.

Put some vinegar on me as well, he thought, and pour some of your drink over me if you want. I won't mind. Just make me feel part of what's going on so I can feel loved.

No one did, though, because it suddenly started to rain. Really hard.

'I don't believe it,' said Dad. 'Come on, everyone, inside!'

The children grabbed their teddies once more and raced towards the back door. Someone scooped up the blanket on which the wooden camel was lying.

He felt his feet slipping.

He was falling, falling.

Down, down.

His face hit the side of the hard concrete of the patio as he fell and his cart crashed down on top of him. Then a small foot kicked him and he skidded into the fence.

At first he was not sure what had happened. There was noise and feet and then the back door closed with a thud and there was nothing except the rain drumming on the concrete slab where he lay.

He was wet and cold and his face hurt where he had fallen.

I can't cry, he thought, because I'm made out of wood, but the rain is like my tears and I'm crying for you, Helen. You wanted me to smile but I know I never will because they don't love me. They didn't really want me at their party. I was brought out by mistake and they haven't even noticed I'm missing.

He lay there for a long, long time. Darkness crept over the garden and a chill wind set in. He heard the children leave as

the party ended and watched as the children's mum pulled down the blinds at the kitchen window. It was going to be a long, dark night.

Suddenly the back door was thrown open and Simon burst into the garden.

'I'm not going to bed until I've found him,' he announced. 'He's one of my most favouritest toys and I don't care if I get wet. I'm going to look for him.'

Must have lost his teddy, the wooden camel thought. I didn't know there was someone else out here as well as me in this rain.

Then he brightened up.

Maybe they would find him while they were looking.

Lottie came out with Dad. He had a torch and an umbrella and moved slowly across the garden swinging the beam of light from side to side. The wooden camel winced as the light fell on his face.

'Found him,' Dad called out.

'Oh no,' he said. 'A bit of wood's broken off his mouth. It must have happened when he was dropped.'

The wooden camel felt himself being picked up and then put in Simon's waiting arms. It was like that first time Helen had held him by the stall in the market. Her arms had been gentle and she had wanted to look after him. Simon's arms were like that now, and what was it Simon had said a few minutes ago about looking for one of his favourite toys? He must have been talking about...

The wooden camel looked up at Simon's face. It was smiling down at him. And in that moment a warm, happy feeling, like the one he had lost so long ago, started to grow in his tummy. It spread all over him. Like when you know you are loved.

'See where that bit of wood's chipped off his mouth,' Dad said as they took him inside. 'It almost looks as if he's smiling now.'

Simon looked closely at the precious toy in his arms, and the rather special little wooden camel simply smiled back at him.

Why is it important to let other people know that you love them?

'...so they don't get lonely...'

'...because it makes it better for them to love you back...'

'...it's nice to know someone loves you.
My mum tells me sometimes.
My brother doesn't but I don't like him anyway...'

'...it's soppy...'

Other things children have said

'...sometimes someone thinks about you and after a bit they stop. But I still love him even if he doesn't come and see me any more...'

'...everyone is important to someone...'

Thinking time

Think of one person you love.

○ How do you show that you love them?

○ How do other people show that they
love you?

○ What does it feel like to be loved?

○ If you were to say one thing about each person
in this room that showed why you liked
being with them, what would it be?

Prayers

Dear God, thank you for all the people who love us and show that they care for us. Amen

Dear God, these are people who I love

....

....

....

Thank you for them. Amen

Dear God, sometimes it's hard to tell someone we love them. Help us to think about different ways we can show our love. Amen

Dear God, thank you that it does not matter what we look like, or where we live, or what clothes we wear, or how we speak, or who our friends are, or where we were born. Thank you that you love us for what we are. Help us to love other people like that as well. Amen

Bullying

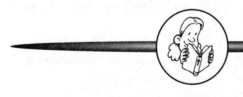

Jesus said to those who believed in him, 'If you obey my teaching, you are really my disciples; you will know the truth, and the truth will set you free.'

John 8:31–32

O God... I come to you for safety.
In the shadow of your wings I find protection
until the raging storms are over.

Psalm 57:1

If something is happening that you do not like, it makes you unhappy inside. You might even be nasty to other people as you try to protect yourself from whatever is making you so sad.

If you are being bullied, you may have to be very brave and tell someone about it, especially if you have been told *not* to tell anyone. In the end, telling the truth is always best. Telling God helps and can be the first step to improving the situation.

Psalm 57 says that believing in God is like looking for, and then finding, safety while a storm is going on.

Spid became nasty because it seemed to be the only way to survive in the dark wood. Then something happened.

The wellies

Spid was a beautiful spider with fine, silky fur all over her body and long, strong legs.

It was a Monday when she arrived in the wood.

The first things she noticed were the brightly coloured wellies. They were not making any noise or anything like that. They were just there, next to her.

All eight of them.

As it was not raining, she decided they could stay where they were. She could always come back for them later if need be— after she had explored the wood.

The grass tickled her furry little legs as she scuttled through the undergrowth. She liked the feel of it. Up over little stones she went, under soft green leaves, round tiny clumps of toad-stools and little flowers, until she came to a clearing where she stopped to draw breath.

She felt alive, happy and free as she arched her back so the warm sun could rest on it.

All I need now is a friend, she thought. I hope I find one soon.

Why do we need friends?

'...so you don't get lonely...'

'...it's always better if there's someone you know when you go to somewhere new...'

'...you can help each other if one of you gets into trouble. You can look after each other...'

'...my friends are nasty to me sometimes...'

At that moment there was a rustling in the grass behind her.

'Hello,' Spid said, turning to see who it was, 'I've just arrived here and my name's Spid. Would you like to be my frie...?'

She stopped as an enormous shadow blocked out the sun and a pair of black wellies ground to a halt in front of her. They belonged to a rather large beetle.

'I don't need anyone, let alone a friend,' it spat at her.

'Why not?' Spid asked.

'Because friends always let you down.'

'I wouldn't,' Spid said. She could not imagine what life must be like without friends.

'You would,' the beetle said. 'You'd be like everyone else. Now get out of my way you stupid, pathetic, pea-brained, scum-bagged little spider.' It kicked one of its front wellies at Spid, then disappeared into the long grass.

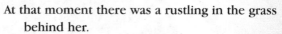

Why was the beetle so nasty to Spid?

'...because it's a nasty beetle...' '...it hasn't got any friends...'

'...he had a friend once, only the friend let him down and now he doesn't need them...'

Spid stayed where she was for a few minutes clutching her throbbing face until the pain began to ease off. There was a noise like someone sniffing. She looked up to see who it was.

A big spider was leaning against a stone at the edge of the

clearing, watching her. He, too, wore wellies. Black, muddy ones, like the beetle's.

'If you've just arrived in this wood you've got a lot to learn, haven't you?' he said.

'Have I?' Spid said.

'Why haven't you got your wellies on, for a start?' he asked her.

'Because it wasn't raining,' Spid whispered back.

'Oh dear,' he sneered. 'You're very small, aren't you, and a bit stupid. Spid the kid with a face like a dustbin lid. Huh! In this wood wellies aren't for keeping the rain out.'

'What are they for then?'

The big spider shrugged his shoulders.

'To stop you being hurt some of the time and to kick out at others the rest. Like that beetle did to you just then. Makes you feel big when you lash out, especially when you find someone who's scared of you. But I'll tell you something, seeing as you're new round here. If you're going to smash someone up, make sure they're not going to tell someone else about it. Because if they *do* go telling, you could get into big, and I mean, big, trouble yourself. Have you got that?'

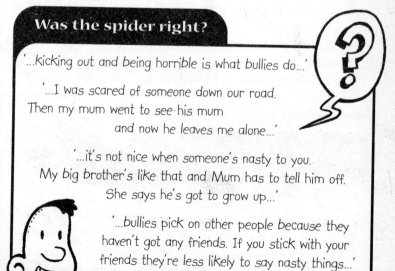

Was the spider right?

'...kicking out and being horrible is what bullies do...'

'...I was scared of someone down our road. Then my mum went to see his mum and now he leaves me alone...'

'...it's not nice when someone's nasty to you. My big brother's like that and Mum has to tell him off. She says he's got to grow up...'

'...bullies pick on other people because they haven't got any friends. If you stick with your friends they're less likely to say nasty things...'

73

'So where *are* your wellies?' the big spider asked again.

'Back there,' Spid said, pointing to the direction she had come from.

'And I suppose they're all bright colours?' he asked, and started laughing when Spid nodded. A bitter, nasty laugh.

'All wellies are like that to start with,' he said. 'They'll soon go black like everyone else's. You'll see.'

Spid suddenly remembered about wanting a friend. The big spider was on his own, so maybe he had not got a friend and would be hers and they could go round together.

'Would you be my friend?' she asked him.

The big spider said nothing for a minute. Then he lowered his head and walked towards her. Spid waited, wondering what he was going to do.

'Push off,' he spat when he reached her. 'In this wood no one has friends.'

For a brief moment, Spid and the big spider stared at one another. Spid saw the hard, sad expression on the spider's face before she turned and began to run.

Was the big spider a friend or a bully?

'...if he'd been a friend he would have told
her to go back home and come and find him if
the beetle was nasty to her again...'

74

'...a bully because he made Spid feel
small and sad and then he hurt her...'

'...he was nice to her at the beginning then he upset her...'

'...a friend would have helped her be brave and stand up to
the beetle but he didn't and then he became a bully as
well. Some friends can bully you sometimes...'

Spid found her wellies and gave them a hug. No
miserable old black ones for her. She had something far better and she was not going to let them
go black.

The pair with red and yellow stripes went on her front legs,
the ones with green and gold spots were second, followed by
the ones with silver and turquoise circles. The blue and pink
diamonds went at the back. They looked fantastic. Maybe wearing wellies would not be so bad after all.

She thought about the beetle and the spider and how nasty
they had been to her.

Was everyone in this beautiful wood like them? she wondered.

She hoped not, yet she did not want anyone else being horrible to her. So what could she do?

In the end she decided to hide if anyone came near her, just
in case. She would leave finding a friend until later.

And with that she set off once more. The wellies got in the
way a bit and she could not run like she had before. But they
were quite soft and comfortable and she definitely felt safer in
them. And they would be *very* useful if it came on to rain.

Spid enjoyed her day. She managed to hide when she heard
wellies approaching—apart from when she nearly tripped over
a tiny beetle herself. He was resting by a patch of daisies in the
middle of an open patch of ground. *His* wellies were bright
green and pink. He looked rather sweet in them.

'Ooh!' he said in a high-pitched voice, then scuttled off out
of sight.

There were so many new and exciting things to find out about that she forgot how awful the beetle and big spider had been. One thing puzzled her, though, and that was the huge wall. Whichever direction she travelled in, she always came to it. She tried to climb over it at first, but it was covered with something so slippery that she always ended up sliding back down again, before she had reached the top.

Is this wall here to keep everyone in, or to keep something out? she wondered.

By the time evening came, Spid was very tired. She found a nice leaf to curl up under and settled down. She breathed in deeply, closed her eyes and began to go to sleep. Tomorrow she would start looking for a friend.

'I'll rip your legs off one by one if you don't move,' a voice snarled at her.

Spid opened her eyes as a shudder of fear ran through her.

The snail, his whole body covered in one thick, black wellie towered above, staring down at her. It was a nasty, vicious stare. Not friendly at all.

'Look at you,' it sneered. 'You're so frightened.'

Spid did not wait to hear more. Trembling all over, she started to run. She ran and ran and ran, as fast as her wellied legs would carry her. She did not care where she went. All she wanted to do was get away.

She did not see the hole that was waiting for her, and twisted on to her back as she fell. Down, down she went until she lay in a pile of dust at the bottom.

'Why is everyone nasty to me?' she sobbed. 'All I want is a friend. Someone I can trust and who likes me because I'm me.'

Her tears trickled down her face and as each one fell it rolled on to her wellies, and began washing them. Soon the shine came off and then the colours began to fade and, before long, the red and yellow stripes, green and gold spots, silver and turquoise circles and pink and blue diamonds had completely disappeared, washed away by her tears.

And in the darkness, Spid carried on crying.

'...bullying...'

'...the beetle saying nasty things in a nasty voice...'

'...because she was nice underneath and everyone around her was horrible and she doesn't really want to be horrible because she's not like that really...'

'...she kept being told to go away and she didn't have any friends, and that was all she wanted, only they wouldn't be her friend and she didn't know why...'

'...they were all so nasty to her...'

At last there were no tears left and Spid fell asleep. Night passed and dawn brought a new day with it. Spid woke up and crawled out of the hole.

'Right,' she said, 'this is a new day and I'm going...'

Then she stopped, staring at her wellies. They were hard and uncomfortable. She tried to shake them off, but they wouldn't move. They were completely stuck to her legs and, worst of all, they had become... black.

The more Spid stared at her wellies, the angrier and crosser she became. All thoughts of trying to find a friend or exploring the wood were gone, for someone had taken her beautiful, soft wellies away and left these horrible black ones instead.

It was at that moment that the unfortunate little caterpillar appeared. He was a vivid pink colour with gorgeous long black hair that stuck up. On his feet were loads of pairs of brightly coloured wellies. Each one of them was a different colour and he loved them. He had been trying to eat a dead leaf and had just decided that soft green ones tasted better than the brown crunchy ones.

'Hello,' he said to Spid in a chirpy voice. 'I've just arrived here and I'm finding out about the wood. Do you want to come and join me?'

Spid stared at him. How dare this little caterpillar speak to her like that? How dare he be happy when she was not? How dare he wear those wellies that were so bright, when hers were black?

She lowered her head and spat at him, nearly blowing him over. Then she laughed out loud and made fun of his pink colour and called him rude names, watching with delight as his face crumpled and he started to cry. One of his tears rolled down the outside of his front right wellie, and the gold and red spots now had a black line through them where the colours had been washed away.

Isn't it wonderful? Spid thought. He's scared of me. He's little and I'm big.

Then she kicked him as hard as she could. He cried out in pain, so she lashed out again, just for fun, then told him to get lost.

Spid was part of the wood now. She was showing them she could survive and nobody need ever know how much she was hurting, deep inside, and how she had once wanted a friend.

She found a nice patch of soft moss under an overgrown bush and made it her own. It was by the big oak tree to the left-hand side of the path and she was rarely disturbed there. Anyway, she saw anyone off who did come visiting.

She did not need friends, so she thought, and if something had not happened, Spid would have spent the rest of her days living there, on her own.

But that was not to be, for other things had been planned.

It was a Saturday when it happened.

The day started like all the rest. The sun rose, the dew on the grass glistened and Spid poked her nose out from under the bush. There was something in the air that morning. A strange crackling noise as well. She sniffed. What was it?

Suddenly she knew what it was.

Fire!

She scuttled on to the path and gasped as a wall of hazy heat greeted her.

She had to get away. Fast.

She raced along the path as quickly as she could, her heart pounding and straining as she tried to go faster, faster, but her wellies kept getting in the way. They were too heavy, too cumbersome. She could hardly spin a web in them, let alone escape from flames that were flickering not far behind her.

Eventually she had to stop to catch her breath and it was as she lay, gasping for breath, that she remembered the wall. There was no way of getting over it, was there?

'What am I going to do?' she cried, then whispered, 'No one will miss me anyway, so what does it matter?'

'I'd miss you,' a voice said.

Spid looked up. A person was sitting with his back against a broken tree stump just in front of her.

'I'd miss you,' he calmly said again, looking straight back at her.

'Who are you?' Spid said.

She wondered what on earth he was doing, sitting with his back against a tree stump that was about to be destroyed by scorching flames. Didn't he know there was a fire? Couldn't he feel the heat and hear the roaring noise it was making?

'I'm the owner of the wood,' he replied rather sadly. Spid had to listen really carefully to catch what he said.

'You're the owner,' she repeated, just to make sure she had heard him correctly.

He nodded.

If he *was* the owner, she thought, maybe he could help her.

'How do I get out, then?' she asked. 'How do I get over that wall you've put all the way round it?'

He sighed.

'I didn't build that wall,' he said. 'This wood used to be such a beautiful place, then you all decided to wear wellies, and you built that wall. I made a hole in it a while back so you could escape, but not many of you found it.'

'Bet I can find it!' Spid shouted up at him.

'But you don't know where it is, do you?' he answered.

'I'll manage,' Spid said and began to move on.

'How will you find it?' he asked as she drew level with his feet.

Spid stopped and they stared at each other while she tried to think of an answer.

'I don't know,' she finally whispered.

'I could tell you where it is if you wanted me to,' he said, 'but I'm not shouting above the roar of these flames. You'll have to let me pick you up so we can talk properly.'

Spid was not sure she wanted to be picked up just then. She really wanted to be on her way. Yet she *had* to find out where the hole was, otherwise she would be burnt alive.

He had put his hand on the ground for her to climb on to so he could pick her up.

She gasped when she saw it. The fingers were all right but the rest was damaged. The skin was lumpy and scarred and it looked as if something had been pushed right through all the bones.

He seemed to know what she was thinking.

'I was wounded while I was making the hole in the wall,' he said. 'It's all right, it doesn't hurt any more.'

'Oh,' she said.

'You've got to take your wellies off,' he said once she was level with his nose. 'Then you can run faster.'

'But you have to wear wellies in this wood,' Spid said.

'I don't wear any,' he replied.

Spid peered over the side of his hand. He was right. He did not wear wellies.

His feet were damaged too, like his hands. They were going to get damaged again if he did not hurry up.

They would be burnt.

So would hers.

The fire was about twelve trees away now and sparks were floating in the air. Spid watched a clump of thistles being reduced to nothing in a couple of seconds.

'We're running out of time,' the owner said softly.

Yes, Spid thought. We are. Why was he wasting time by telling her to take her wellies off when she knew she couldn't because they were stuck to her legs? Why didn't he just tell her where the hole in the wall was?

'My wellies are sort of part of me,' Spid said.

Why are Spid's wellies so important to her?

'...they stop other animals hurting her...'

'...they make her feel big so she can smash up other little animals like the ones that are smaller than what she is...'

'...they stop her running fast...'

'...she doesn't really like them because she liked them at first when they were all bright colours but then they went black...'

'...she liked them because she could be a bully in them, especially if she could find someone who didn't have any wellies on at all...'

'They won't come off anyway,' she added.

She was filled with a longing to escape, to get away, to start again. To have friends she could trust, friends who did not wear black wellies.

She suddenly said, 'Can *you* pull them off for me?'

The owner smiled at her. Spid found herself smiling back. It was the first time she had ever smiled a real smile, but it faded quickly as he began to tug at one of her front wellies.

It hurt.

It hurt a lot, and Spid screamed out as he pulled.

'You're hurting me,' she cried.

81

'I know, but I have to get you out of these wellies,' he said gently.

'What colour were they before they went black?' he asked.

'I've forgotten,' she whispered. 'I know I liked them, though. They were really pretty.'

'Those ones were red with yellow stripes,' he said and chuckled to himself. The last time Spid had seen her front legs they had been soft, furry and a dull sort of brown colour. Now they were still soft, they were still furry, but they had become the most exquisite shade of red with bright yellow stripes going from top to bottom.

'Let's see what else those wellies are covering up,' he said and began pulling the others off, one by one.

'My beautiful little friend,' he whispered as the last one was removed.

Spid looked down at the array of turquoise and silver and red and yellow and green and gold and pink and blue beneath her. She *was* beautiful, and she trembled with pleasure as she stood there in the palm of his hand.

Very gently he lowered her to the ground. The grass tickled her legs as it had when she'd first arrived in the wood. It felt even lovelier now.

'See that path,' he showed her. 'You'll come to the hole in the wall if you go down there.'

Spid looked in amazement. She had never seen the path before.

'Thank you,' she shouted out at the top of her voice.

She had to shout to get above the noise of the fire. It was so close now, but she was not worried. At last her legs were free and she was able to run fast and escape.

'Where are you going?' she asked him.

'Around,' he said, and smiled at her again. 'Just around. Now off you go.'

Spid did not need telling twice. She was off, down the path to freedom.

The owner stood up as Spid went. He took the black wellies in his hands and threw them deep, deep into the fire. Spid's

were not the only ones he had taken off that day. Neither would they be the last.

Like the others, the wellies melted and bubbled and sizzled until they were no more.

What colour would your wellies be?

'...different blues with yellow spots...'

'...lavender and yellow...'

'...white with little gold stars on...'

'...elephant shapes with white circles all round them...'

'...yellow with *blue bobbles* that light up...'   '...zig zags...'

'...pink with *beautiful teddy bears* all over them...'

'...turquoise, my favourite colour...'

'...I'd never ever want to have *black* ones on because they're the sort that *bullies* wear...'

Other things children have said

'...bullies are sad people because they are being bullied as well and that's why they have to bully us...'

'...people have black wellies so they can hide better...'

'...bullies always wear black wellies...'

Thinking time

Think about a time when you have been
hurt and upset by someone.

- Did you tell anyone about it?
- Have you got over it

   or does it still upset you?

- What would you do if it happened again?

Prayers

Dear God, if I am sad about
something, please help me to tell
someone. Thank you that I can always tell
you about anything and you will still love me. Amen

Dear God, I'm being bullied by ....
I've thought about it and this is the person I want to tell
.... Help me to know when is the
best time for me to talk to them about it. Help me to be
really brave and tell them everything. Amen

Dear God, I'm going to tell you the name of someone
who is always being nasty to me ....
Please show me what to do about it. Amen

Dear God, someone I know keeps being nasty to me.
Help me stand up for myself and to try to be nice to them
at the same time. It's very difficult to do. Amen

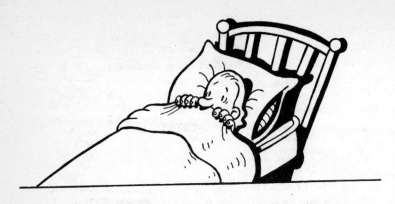

Being scared is OK

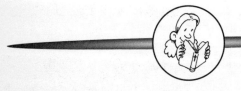

We know that in all things God works for good
with those who love him.

Romans 8:28

When I am afraid, O Lord Almighty, I put my trust in
you... You know how troubled I am; you have kept a
record of my tears... I walk in the presence of God, in
the light that shines on the living.

Psalm 56:3, 8 and 13

One of the underlying themes of the Bible is that God is with us when we are afraid and will bring good out of bad situations. It can help to remember this when things are troubling us and good things seem to be a long, long way away.

The poem is about someone who is feeling scared.

I'm scared

Sometimes
I'm scared
When I lie in my bed
On my own
In the dark.
Why?
Because sometimes
My head is full
Of the things
I don't like to think about.
Am I ever going to get to sleep?
Or will I lie here,
Wide awake,
And scared
All night?
I wish I were older.
Then I'd stay up longer.
But I have to go to bed
On my own
In the dark.
In my head are
Scary things I've seen on TV,
Scary things I've seen in books.
Something someone said to me,
Scary words and
Scary looks.
Sometimes I don't understand
And sometimes I felt silly
Because I should

Have known
What they were talking about.
Only I didn't.
'Try to get to sleep,' says Mum
When I tell her.
Only she doesn't remember
What it is like
To be little
In a great big world.

In my head are
Scary narrow pavements
With gi-normous lorries rumbling by
And the horrid, smelly dog that barks
Behind the big black gate
That we have to walk past
On the way to school.
And I don't like it
Because one day,
That
Dog
Might
Jump over the gate
And get me.
There are loads of other things
Which I'm trying not to think about
And I want to go to sleep,
But
I don't want any nightmares
About all the scary things
That are in my head.
That's why
Sometimes
I'm scared
When I lie in my bed
On my own
In the dark.
Am I ever going to get to sleep?

Things children have said about being scared

...about the dark

'...I don't like the shadows my night-light makes...'

'...there's a door to our loft outside my bedroom door and I think there's a nasty man up there with a knife and he wants to get me...'

'...if I need a toilet in the middle of the night and I have to go downstairs I always think there's a robber in our sitting-room and he's going to get me as I go past the door. I run dead quick until I get there...'

'...if I'm on the top bunk I'm scared I'll fall out and hurt myself. I did once and my mum got cross with me...'

'...you don't know what's going on in the dark. It might be nasty. You just don't know...'

'...kidnappers come out at night and might take me away and hurt me...'

'...we go shopping in the dark sometimes and I have to hold on to the buggy and walk next to the bushes. I always think someone's going to jump out of the bushes and get me and my mum will look after the baby and leave me alone...'

'...I'm sure there's a monster lurking behind my door. I hate my bedroom door because it stops me being part of the rest of the house...'

...about bathrooms

'...I used to think there was a monster who

lived down the toilet and he would come up
and bite my bottom if I sat on it too long...'

'...when you turn on our taps in the bathroom, the water
squirts all over the place and that scares me...'

'...my nanny gets spiders in her bath. I always
have a shower when I'm there...'

'...we have a fan that comes on in our bathroom and
I think it looks at me as it goes round...'

...about things seen on screens

'...my mum doesn't always let me watch the things
she does. She says they'll scare me...'

'...I thought there was an alien with green eyes in my
bedroom after I watched a film once. My mum told me
to stop being so stupid but she hadn't seen the film
because I watched it at Kevin's house...'

'...I imagined there was zombies sucking blood out of
my neck because that's what they do on my new computer
game. I didn't tell my mum or dad because they would
have taken the game away from me and I still wanted to
play it even though it scared me...'

...about cupboards

'...the door creaks when you open it...'

'...our airing-cupboard scares me because it's
got a big red thing inside it that makes all funny noises.
I hear it when I'm trying to go to sleep. I think it might
explode and pour boiling hot water all over me...'

...about parents

'...when he gets cross I get really
scared in case he starts throwing things at me...'

'...my mum says she's going to the sitting-room
when I'm trying to go to sleep. But I know she's not
because I hear her in the kitchen. She's told me
a lie and she shouldn't do that...'

...about robbers

'...my friend's house had robbers
and I thought it might happen to us...'

'...if a robber came in my house he might wear a mask
and I don't like people wearing masks because you can't see
their faces and they might hurt me...'

...about the wind

'...it's stronger than me. It might knock me over
and I'd hurt myself...'

...about people

'...if my friends break up with me I have no one to
protect me in the playground...'

'...when they're bigger than me and I know
they're going to be nasty to me even though
I've told my mummy about them...'

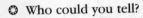

Thinking time

Often the first step
to making things we are scared about go
away is to tell someone about them.
Is there something or someone who
scares you at the moment?

- Who could you tell?
- When could you tell them?
- What would you say?

Prayers

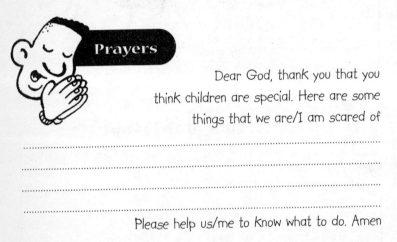

Dear God, thank you that you
think children are special. Here are some
things that we are/I am scared of

....

....

....

....

Please help us/me to know what to do. Amen

Dear God, when I'm scared, help me to be
really sensible and face up to the thing I don't like.
Help me to understand my fear. Amen

Dear God, help me remember that
you are always with me wherever I go. Amen

Racial issues

God says, 'I do not judge as people judge. They look at the outward appearance, but I look at the heart.'

1 Samuel 16:7

We often put a lot of store on the way people look and where they come from, rather than who they are deep inside. The Bible reminds us that God doesn't take any notice of outward appearance; it's what's inside that matters. Jesus illustrates this point in his parable about the Good Samaritan, which you can read in Luke 10:25–37. In Jesus' day, the people of Samaria were treated badly, simply because of where they came from. Jesus shows us that it's the way we behave towards other people that really matters.

In the story, Siguna goes to a new school where he finds he is very different from all the other children.

We're all different

'I've put my tooth under the pillow,' Siguna said. 'Are you sure the tooth fairy will be able to find me?'

'Of course she will,' Mither replied. 'Now, try and get some sleep. You've got a busy day ahead of you.'

She bent over and gave him a kiss.

I hope everything's all right tomorrow, she thought.

For tomorrow, Siguna was going to a new school.

Siguna closed his eyes. The next thing he knew, sunlight was streaming through the curtains and it was morning. He slid his hand under his pillow.

The tooth fairy *had* been.

Brilliant!

'I shall buy some sweets with this tonight,' he whispered, clutching a silver coin in his hand, 'to give to my new friends.'

He got out of bed and went to find Mither. They had breakfast together and then Mither took out some face paints and painted Siguna's face and hands a light brown colour. The brush tickled and he began giggling.

'You look like you've been in the sun now,' Mither laughed when she had finished. 'We'll just do this for a couple of days, until everyone at school gets used to you.'

Why did Mither paint Siguna's face and hands?

'...she doesn't want anyone to see his hands or his head...'

'...all the other people in the school are brown and he wants to be like them...'

'...if he looks like he's come from abroad they'll all be much nicer to him and look after him better. That's what I'd do, anyway...'

Siguna held Mither's hand very tightly as they walked across the playground.

'They're all looking at me,' he whispered.

'They're probably thinking how nice it's going to be to get to know you,' Mither whispered back.

'Are they?' Siguna asked in an even quieter whisper.

He hoped they were.

So did Mither.

Mither and Siguna had a chat with the head teacher before he was taken across to his new classroom. The teacher looked up and smiled as he came through the door. Siguna liked her straight away. She had long brown hair and bright red nail varnish on her fingernails. Her name was Mrs Jennings.

When you see someone for the first time, what do you notice about them?

'...how friendly they look...'

'...if their hands have got little wrinkles on them like my gran has...'

'...their shoes, if they're posh or shiny or high...'

'...their voice, how deep and loud
and if they have an accent or not...'

'...the colour of their skin...'

'...if they smile at me or not...'

'...what clothes they are wearing...'

Mrs Jennings took Siguna to a table where several children were sitting.

'Jane and Sam will look after you today,' she said kindly. 'There's your chair and you've got a drawer under the table. I've done a label with your name on already. We're just about to get ready for PE.'

Siguna went cold all over.

Not PE.

Anything but PE.

Not on the first lesson of the first day in a new place. It was not that he was useless at PE. Siguna loved it, and was great at doing handstands and climbing ropes and playing football. It was just that he did not, under any circumstance whatsoever, want to take his jumper off.

Not today, anyway.

'Don't worry if you haven't got anything to change into,' Mrs Jennings said and gave him a plastic bag. 'There's a spare T-shirt and some shorts in there you can use.'

Siguna took out the T-shirt and carefully laid it on the table. He glanced over his shoulder to see if anyone was watching. They all seemed to be busy talking to each other and getting changed themselves so he lifted his jumper up really fast, pulled it over his head and reached out for the T-shirt, struggling to get it on as quickly as he could.

Too slow!

'That new boy's got green skin!' someone gasped.

There was laughing and giggling behind him as other children crowded round to have a look. Siguna felt someone touch his back. Then another finger prodded his skin.

'Bet he smells,' someone whispered. 'Fancy having green skin.'

Siguna wished he were back home.

'Does it matter?' he wanted to shout out. 'I'm still a person and I have feelings and I hurt when you stare at me and whisper about me and touch my back. I was born with green skin and I can't change that and… and…'

But he did not even open his mouth.

Siguna simply pulled the T-shirt down and sat in his seat, looking at the table. The tear that rolled down his cheek washed a line through the face paint, showing more green skin underneath. He wiped the tear away with the back of his hand and the paint on his hand became smudged as well as that on his face.

I wish my skin was the same as everyone else's, he thought.

Mrs Jennings came over and put her arm round him.

'I can't believe what's just happened,' she said.

'I want to go home,' Siguna whispered. 'Please let me.'

'You've got to stick it out,' Mrs Jennings said. 'But I'm going to help you, because I think this lot have been horrible and I'm ashamed of them.'

She did not give Siguna chance to answer before she stood up.

'Line up.' She spat the words out. Her voice was not kind or friendly any more, but harsh and angry. 'Maybe by the end of this PE lesson you'll all have learned something important,' she barked.

They walked across to the hall in silence. Siguna held Mrs Jennings' hand and stayed by her as everyone got out the large PE apparatus. There was a huge climbing-frame and ropes and rope ladders and plastic tunnels to climb through; much more than had been at Siguna's last school.

In one corner, Mrs Jennings told some of the children to put out four large mats.

'What are they for?' someone asked.

'You'll find out,' came the cross reply. Then everyone was given a coloured band. Five were blue, all the others were red.

The children were then allowed on the apparatus. They could go anywhere they wanted to.

'Do you want to go on the apparatus?' Mrs Jennings asked Siguna.

'No,' he whispered and shook his head. He felt safe by the teacher.

'Stay here with me then,' Mrs Jennings said, and gave him a sad, gentle smile.

Why is Mrs Jennings sad for Siguna?

'...because he hasn't got any friends...'

'...because he's got green skin and no one else has and they've been nasty to him because he's different to them...'

'...she's looking after him...'

'...she wants to help Siguna be happy in school. That's what her job is...'

'All children with red bands, sit on the mats, please,' she suddenly announced. 'Blue bands stay on the apparatus.'

Blue bands, of course, thought this was wonderful and climbed and swung on the ropes while the others had to watch.

A few minutes later, Mrs Jennings produced a packet of chocolate biscuits from her bag.

'Anyone with a blue band, come and get a biscuit,' she said.

'What about us?' one of the children on the mats called out.

'You're wearing red bands so you don't count,' she snapped and then ignored them.

The five blue-band children sat down until they had finished their biscuits, then went back on the apparatus again. They were having a lovely time and began pulling faces and laughing at those on the mats.

'How do we become blues?' someone asked.

'You can't,' Mrs Jennings said. 'Once you're a red, you're always a red and that's that. Now be quiet.'

'Why are you being nice to them and not us?' someone else asked a few minutes later.

'I'm just letting you know how Siguna must have felt this morning,' Mrs Jennings said in a cold voice.

'It's not fair them getting all the goes on the apparatus,' someone started to say.

'Be quiet,' Mrs Jennings snapped.

There was silence for several minutes, apart from the noise of five children climbing on the apparatus. Then the blue bands were asked to join the red ones on the mats.

'It's not very nice when some people are treated differently, is it?' Mrs Jennings said to them all. 'But that is how you treated Siguna this morning. You laughed at him and talked about him behind his back. I was appalled with the way you behaved. It doesn't matter what colour anyone's skin is, or where they come from, or what language they speak, they are still the same as you and they hurt inside when you are nasty to them. Every single one of you is special and loved just because you are you.'

The children stared at her. She did not get angry very often.

'I think,' Mrs Jennings carried on, 'we'll start this lesson again. In a minute you can take your bands off. Then anyone with freckles can go on the climbing-frame, and those who normally wear glasses can use the rope ladders…'

It was then that Siguna heard something that made his hair stand on end with happiness.

'What do you want?' Mrs Jennings asked the boy who had put his hand up.

'Can Siguna be in my group?' he said.

'That would be lovely,' Mrs Jennings said and smiled. 'But which group will it be? We've had freckles and glasses.'

'What about those with a front tooth missing?' someone suggested and everyone, including Siguna, laughed out loud.

'Brilliant,' their teacher said, 'and that group can go and work where the benches and hoops are.'

Other things children have said

'...you should like yourself.
People that laugh at you are sad themselves...'

'...it doesn't matter what you look like on the outside.
You could have freckles or spots or anything.
It's what you're like inside that's important.
That's what I think anyway...'

'...people who are nasty to other people
are horrible themselves...'

'...You mustn't listen if someone says something you don't like.
You must ignore them, then they go away. Only they don't
always. Then you have to tell a grown-up, like a teacher or
a dinner lady or your mum or dad and they have to do
something about it. If they don't they're letting you down...'

Thinking time

Has anyone ever done anything nasty to you because you were different to them?

- ☺ What did it feel like?

- ☺ Are you still upset about it?

- ☺ How can you try to stop it happening again?

Have *you* ever been nasty to someone?

⚙ What did it feel like?

⚙ Did you like it when they got upset?

⚙ Would you upset them again?

⚙ Why?

Prayers

Dear God, we're all different and that is how you made us. Sometimes people are nasty though, and laugh and say horrible things. Please help me to know what to do if that happens again. Amen

Dear God, when people are different to me it's hard sometimes not to stare at them and talk about them. I know that's not a nice thing to do, so please help me not to do it. Amen

Dear God, thank you that we are all different and that you love each one of us just the same. Amen

Gender issues

You are the people of God; he loved you and chose you for his own. So then, you must clothe yourselves with compassion, kindness, humility, gentleness and patience. Be tolerant with one another and forgive one another… just as the Lord has forgiven you.

Colossians 3:12–13

Each of us is special whether we are male or female, and the Bible tells us that men and women were made to be friends and companions for each other. This means, as this passage from Paul's letter to the church at Colossae shows, that we have to think about the needs of others before we think of our own needs. This is not always easy to do.

At the time when Jesus lived on earth, men thought they were more important than women. Jesus did not agree with this because he saw *every* person as being special.

When people put the needs of others first, very special things can happen, as the two teams in this story, one boys and one girls, found out. They had a competition to raise money for the street children in Guatemala. But who was the real winner?

Teamwork

Early one Saturday, thirteen people met at Amersham railway station. They were going to spend their day travelling on trains on the London Underground network. Every station they went through would help raise money for children who live on the streets of Guatemala in Central America.

NORTH AMERICA

SOUTH AMERICA

Guatemala

Many children in Guatemala have been abandoned by their parents and have to beg or steal food and clothes to survive. The money the two teams raised would go towards building a new house for some of these children to live in.

'I've got twenty-two sponsors,' Sally said. 'Dad took my form to work and got lots of people to sponsor me.'

'I only managed five,' Kate sighed, 'but it'll be all right as long as we go to over one hundred and fifty stations. Mum's promised me £100 if we do, but if we go to less, she's going to give me a fiver for the lot.'

'We should make it,' Jane said.

She was in charge of the girls' team. She'd helped with the challenge last year as well, when her team had clocked up one hundred and eighty-five stations by the end of the day.

'Well, we boys are going to go to more stations *and* raise more money than you girls,' Lee sneered.

'No you're not,' Sally said back.

'Oh yeah!' Sam joined in. 'There's six of us in the boys' team and only five of you. So we're bound to win. Boys are better than girls, anyway.'

'Don't start that,' Mike said. He was in charge of the boys' team and gave Lee a disapproving prod to stop him saying anything else. 'We're here to raise money, not decide if boys are better than girls. Now come on, the train's just pulling in.'

Everyone piled on board.

Each of them had a map, and as the train passed through each station they ticked it off the list. Chalfont and Latimer, Chorleywood, Rickmansworth, Moor Park, Northwood and on down the line to Wembley Park.

'Right lads, we're getting off here,' Mike announced, and stood up.

'Are you going north on the Jubilee line to Stanmore?' Jane asked him.

Mike nodded. 'Where are you heading for first?'

'Epping,' Jane said. 'We'll get one of the furthest ones done first.'

Mike grinned.

'Have a nice day, anyway!' he said. 'See you later.'

The doors hissed as they opened and the boys jostled their way off the train.

'Bet we'll beat you,' Lee whispered as he passed the girls.

Sally tried to kick him, only he jumped out of the way.

'I hate boys,' she said as the train pulled out of the station.

Who do you want to win and why?

'...the girls because they're girls...'

'...the boys. They're stronger and better at football and know more about trains...'

'...girls, because I'm one...'

'...don't mind, because they're all just as good as each other. I just want them to get as much money as possible for the children out in Guatemala without any mummies or daddies...'

It was nearly eleven o'clock before the girls reached Epping. By then they had thirty-four stations ticked off.

They had to wait twenty minutes until another train took them back to Woodford and they could tick off the stations on the loop there.

'I'm hungry,' Jo said, taking out her lunch box. She had enough sandwiches to keep them all going right through the day.

'Pity your mum didn't sponsor us for eating sandwiches,' Jane laughed.

Meanwhile, the boys had reached Morden, at the bottom of the Northern line. It was here that Mike began to really embarrass them. He got out a piece of cardboard. On it were the words, 'We're collecting money for street children in Guatemala. Tap my bald head and give generously. Thank you.'

Mike sat on the edge of his seat and held the piece of cardboard so everyone could see it. Joshua and Sam, who were sitting next to him, asked if they could get off the train and go it alone.

'No,' Mike said, 'we're here to raise money as a team, and this is one way of doing it.'

'Wish I'd gone with the others,' Joshua sighed.

'Not the girls! They're wimps!' Sam said, screwing his nose up. 'That reminds me, I heard a good joke last week. Why do women have small feet?'

'I don't know,' Lee joined in. 'Why *do* women have small feet?'

'So they can get closer to the sink!' Sam laughed.

'Eh?' Joshua said. He did not understand it.

'That's all women are for,' Sam said to him. 'To be in the kitchen and wash up and stand by the sink. They're useless at doing anything else. Do you get it now?'

Joshua was not sure whether to laugh or not. His dad spent as much time in the kitchen as his mum did. He was about to say something about it when Mike chipped in.

'That's enough,' he said. 'Those aren't real jokes, they're just you being nasty.'

Do you think Mike is right?

'...yes, they're horrible because they make you embarrassed...'

'...sometimes they can be funny. As long as you don't take them too far...'

'...they make one lot of people look better and they're not really...'

'...they're not really funny but some people think they are...'

'...my mum thinks they're funny *because* she knows they're a load of rubbish...'

'...people are different. They're not better or worse. They're just different...'

Meanwhile, the girls were getting bored.

'Let's play "I-spy",' Jane said. That was even more boring.

The boys were fed up as well and let everyone know about it. They ended up making so much noise that all the other passengers got off and found other carriages to travel in. Then the boys got off themselves and went to a burger bar for a snack. When they returned to the Underground they were armed with straws. They ripped the wrappers from these into little bits, chewed them, and then, when they were sure Mike wasn't looking, loaded the soggy paper into one end of the straws before blowing down the other, taking aim at unsuspecting passengers. It was at this point that the girls got into real trouble because the train they were travelling in broke down, only a few minutes after it had pulled out of Kew Gardens. They were completely stuck. For over an hour.

'I need the loo!' Emma suddenly said.

'So do I!' Sally groaned.

Fortunately, they didn't have to wait much longer until the train lurched forward. But by the time they'd got off at the next station, found a loo and got back on another train, they had lost over one and a half hours.

'We'll never beat the boys now,' Lizzie groaned. 'Why do they have to win? They'll say it's because we're girls and that we're sad and that they're better than us. But they're not better than us. Ever.'

Are boys better than girls?

'...girls are better *because* boys are lazy...'

'...they're both the same in some things. Boys are better at sports, because some boys are stronger, but not all of them. Some girls are stronger than some boys...'

'...men have to go out and earn money for toys and food for the children. If they sat around all day they'd get bored...'

'...boys are boys and girls are girls and that's it. They're the same at some things and different at others. But they're all good at something. None of them are actually better...'

By the end of the day, both teams were fed up. They met up at Baker Street just after seven o'clock to travel back to Amersham together.

The boys had been through one hundred and eighty-nine stations.

The girls only had one hundred and forty-nine ticked off.

'If we hadn't been in a train that broke down, we'd have had loads more stations,' Jane said sadly.

Mike was standing by Kate. She was very quiet.

'What's the matter?' he asked her.

'I didn't get one hundred and fifty stations, so my mum will only give me five pounds,' she said.

'But you're only one off,' Mike said. 'Won't she imagine you've been to an extra one just to get the number up?'

'You don't know my mum,' Kate said. 'There's no way she'll change her mind.' Her voice trailed off. She wanted to cry because she was so tired and so fed up. But she was determined not to in case she got called a cry-baby.

Do girls cry more than boys?

'...yes, because girls are more precious...'

'...boys fight more to get their feelings out that way...'

109

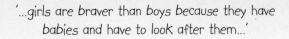

'Shall we count all the stations again and see if you've missed one?' Mike asked. He was really tired himself, but could see Kate was fighting back the tears and wanted to help her.

'All right,' Kate nodded glumly and together they went through the girls' route very carefully. Suddenly Mike jumped up in the air. He had a habit of doing that when he got excited about something.

'You haven't counted Amersham itself, have you?' he said with a huge grin on his face.

Kate looked at him. She looked at her piece of paper. Then she looked back at him again.

He was right!

'That makes one hundred and fifty stations and £100 from my mum,' she said.

'Brilliant!' Mike grinned. 'That's going to make a huge difference to the amount of money your team raises. I expect you'll win now.'

'We won really,' Sam and Lee said together, 'because we went to more stations than the girls did.'

'No you didn't,' Jane said. She was tired of some of the things the boys had been saying. 'The real winners are the children in Guatemala. Because of what both teams have done. So there.'

Other things children have said

...about boys

'fun... stronger... tougher... kind... good-looking... sporty... brilliant... bullies... clever... lazy... friendly...'

...about girls

'silly... sissy... cry-babies... gorgeous... stupid... perfume... clever and intelligent... hard-working...'

'...if you have a brother or a sister you think differently to someone who hasn't got any...'

'...you should all just be friends together...'

Thinking time

- If you think that either boys or girls are better, are you right?
- Why?
- Do you treat some people differently to others because they are either a boy or a girl?
- Is this what you should be doing?

Prayers

Dear God, I like being a boy because............................

....

Thank you for making me one. Amen

Dear God, I like being a girl because..

....

Thank you for making me one. Amen

Dear God, you made us different and we need each other. Help us to know if we say or do something that hurts someone else. Amen

Dear God, to you we are all loved and all equal whether we are male or female. Thank you for this. Amen

Making friends

All who see me jeer at me; they stick out
their tongues and shake their heads.

Psalm 22:7

When I was in trouble, they were all glad
and gathered round to mock me.

Psalm 35:15

Tell them not to speak evil of anyone,
but to be peaceful and friendly, and always to
show a gentle attitude towards everyone.

Titus 3:2

People are not always very kind to each other, but this is not what God wants to happen. He wants us to look after each other and not just ourselves.

When Josie joined a new Brownie pack, she had hoped to make lots of new friends there, only things did not work out how she had hoped they would.

No one to play with

Josie was a Brownie. Where she used to live she went to a Brownie pack that met on Saturday mornings. But Josie's family had had to move when her dad changed his job. Brown Owl said that Josie would be able to join the Wednesday night Brownie pack which met near her new house. When Wednesday came, Josie's mum cooked tea extra early so that Josie could be ready in time.

'I hope you enjoy it,' she said as they walked together to the hall where the Brownie pack met.

Josie smiled. She loved Brownies. She loved the games and learning about different things and making new friends. She just knew she was going to enjoy it.

But Josie was in for a big shock.

The first problem was that she did not know anyone. When she walked into the hall the Brownies were all playing Port and Starboard and she felt shy and alone among so many strange faces. She did not join in. She had known everyone in her old pack.

Josie's new Brown Owl said that she could be in the Kelpies' Six. The Sixer was a girl called Joanne who was supposed to look after her, but Joanne kept forgetting to include her and chatted to her own friends instead. Josie started to feel left out.

They were all working on their bird-watcher badge. Josie did not know what to do. Everyone else did because they had been there last week. Brown Owl explained about making a scrapbook with pictures of birds in and asked Joanne if she could help Josie with hers.

Joanne smiled sweetly and said she would, but soon became engrossed in her own work. She forgot all about Josie and carried on talking to her friends.

There were some books on the table. Josie looked through them and found a picture of a robin. She decided to draw that and found herself a piece of paper. No one had told her to bring a pencil case so she picked up a felt-tipped pen that was lying on the table.

'Oi,' said a cross voice. 'That belongs to the Elves. You Kelpies have your own pens in your Six box.'

'I only wanted to draw my bird,' Josie whispered, putting the felt-tipped pen back.

I really want to go home, she thought.

'...I'd have gone home...'

'...cried, only they might have laughed at me...'

'...hit them *because* they were being *so* horrible to me...'

'...gone and told the person who was in charge...'

Josie flicked through the pages of the bird book. She was not very good at reading and the book had been written for grown-ups, not children, so she could not understand many of the words.

She thought about her old Brownie pack. They always played games before they went home. Maybe they would here. Then she might have a chance to join in.

But when they *did* play games, Josie did not know what to do and let her Six down.

'That new girl's useless,' someone said behind her back as they finished.

My name is Josie, Josie thought, and I'm not useless, it's just that I'm unhappy and want to go home.

'Did you have a good time?' her mum asked as she picked her up.

Josie shook her head and told her what had happened.

Her mum sighed.

Josie lifted her hand and let her fingers curl round Mum's as they walked along.

'You know what,' Mum said.

'What?' Josie asked.

'You could think of everyone at Brownies as being inside a triangle. They all know each other because they've spent quite a bit of time together.'

Josie nodded.

'Now,' Mum carried on, 'imagine them *inside* the triangle and you *outside*.'

'I just never want to go back there again,' Josie said.

'I know,' Mum sighed, 'but that's because you're still on the *outside*. You tried to get inside but the triangle didn't open up to let you in, did it?'

'No one talked to me or let me join in and I think they're all horrid,' Josie said.

They walked in silence for a while, past a little supermarket and then a video shop.

'Tell you what,' said Mum. 'When we get home, I'll sew your new badge on so that everyone knows which Six you're in and then next week we could ask one of the girls to come to tea.

'We could get out a video. Maybe if we do that, and you get to know the others in your Six, the triangle will start to open up,' she added.

'What do you think?'

Josie pulled a face.

'I don't like being on my own,' she said.

'Not many people do,' Mum replied.

Would you go back to the Brownie pack?

'...not if they were horrible to me...'

'...I'd want my mum to say something to the person who was running it and tell them how nasty everyone had been to me the week before...'

'...I'd go once more. You've got to give people a chance when you go somewhere new...'

If you drew a triangle, who would you put inside it?

'...my baby sister and my best friend...'

'...all my friends from school...'

'...everyone because I don't like being outside triangles but I do like being inside them...'

Other things children have said

'...Jane took all my friends and made them play her game and did not let me play so I'm lonely in the playground...'

'...I like John because he is nice to me and cares about me...'

'...I don't like Kevin because sometimes he does not let me play football and then he pushes me over and I hurt myself on the playground...'

'...I dislike Louise because in our road when there is no one to play with she comes and plays with us and we try and be nice to her. But as soon as someone else comes that she likes better she leaves us in the middle of our game and then her mum gets cross with us because she thinks we won't play with her...'

Thinking time

❂ Why do you like to have friends?

❂ Are you always a good friend to them?

❂ What makes a friend into a special friend?

❂ Have you got any special friends?

❂ Why?

Prayers

Dear God, you love us and want us to love other people too. It is hard to do this sometimes and we need your help. Amen

Dear God, thank you for all the friends I have got. May we always get on and if we do fall out with each other to make up again quickly. Amen

Dear God, if someone is outside a triangle and I am inside it, help me to open the triangle up so that person can come inside and be happier. Amen

Further thoughts and additional comments

The following factors are not directly referred to in the stories.

The first experience many children have of death is when a pet dies. It is therefore part of an important learning process.

The child may need to be reassured that he/she was not responsible for the animal's death.

Replacing the animal is an option to consider later on, not necessarily straight away.

Children should be encouraged to take part in a 'funeral service' if that is what they want to do.

Coping with the death of a person is far harder, particularly if they were well-loved.

Whether death was caused by long-term illness or was sudden, the stages of denial, anger and shock will need to be worked through as they surface.

The older the child, the more understanding he/she will have that death is final and cannot be reversed.

All questions need to be answered honestly. Side-tracking from the truth may make it easier for the adult talking to the child, but in the long term does not necessarily help the child.

Some children fear that they, too, might die. This is especially the case if it was a child who died. Concern about their own health may follow.

Treasuring something that belonged to the dead person can be important. This can be for physical comfort or because of a belief that the object will help maintain contact.

Younger children may behave badly because they think they should be punished in some way for the person's death.

Supporting others may be a way of avoiding facing up to the death. It can also be a coping strategy.

Some children need to be given permission to be angry.

A safe place needs to be found for that anger to be fully expressed.

Each child will say 'goodbye' in his/her own way. Grieving continues long after the tears have stopped. It is easy to forget this as 'normal' life resumes.

Maintaining secure, familiar routines is important, as is ensuring the child knows he/she is a loved and valued member of a family and community, where others are also grieving.

Religious faith can give comfort and hope following a bereavement.

Christians believe that God has opened the way for us to live with him in heaven when we die. He does not force people to believe in him if they do not want to. Each person decides while they are alive whether or not they believe in him. This is a private matter between them and God.

The Bible says we shall have new bodies in heaven—spiritual ones that work properly and do not feel pain.

People do not go to heaven and then come back again.

The Bible does not say what happens to animals when they die. What we do know is that God loves everything he makes and therefore cares about animals when they die.

A child's understanding of God depends largely on what has been explained at home, at church, at school and what his/her friends believe.

God is spirit, but he is not a ghost. The Bible specifically tells us not to get involved in the supernatural.

We can talk to God at any time and wherever we are. He will always be there to listen to us.

Children caught up in the breakdown of the family unit may be left feeling powerless.

They may react by trying to control other people, either in or outside the home.

Their parents may use them as pawns, trying to keep the child on 'their' side.

Time set aside for the children may become tense and strained.

Children need to be reminded that they are loved and are not to blame for what has happened as calm, honest answers are given to painful questions.

Once separation is decided upon, it is important to keep the child informed about what will happen to him/her in the future.

Any hope of reconciliation, which many children cling to, fades if a new partner arrives.

If the child shows affection towards a new partner he/she may fear rejection if the parent who is not there finds out how the child feels.

A new partner brings different values, standards and, sometimes, other children.

Moving house is also a possibility. This in itself, without the problems of creating a new family unit, can be a very traumatic as friends and a safe, known environment are left behind.

It is also a busy time for the adults involved.

Making children feel part of proceedings helps. If secrets are kept, anxieties about the future may develop.

Involving children and valuing their input is important to develop the child's self-image.

A good self-image comes when children feel accepted, loved and valued for what they are rather than what they think others want them to be.

A bad self-image develops out of critical relationships which make children feel inadequate and failures. To protect themselves, they may become anxious and defensive, sometimes finding it difficult to make friends.

This can result in physical, verbal or emotional bullying.

Bullies depend on silence.

Victims, and potential victims, must be encouraged to 'tell' what is happening to them and given space to do this in confidence.

They need then to see that something is being done about it.

Adverse comments about race and gender are bullying and need to be treated as such.

Look out for

More stories to make you think

With the proven success of her first book, *Stories to make you think*, Heather Butler now covers a further eleven sensitive issues for 6–10s who find themselves needing to talk. this book includes anger management, abuse, illness, disability and personal hygiene.

The book uses biblical insights and thinking time to provide an accessible entry point into these difficult subjects. Each story has been researched and tested in Circle Time and PHSE at primary level and can be used either in a one-to-one situation or with a group in the classroom, church or family.

ISBN 1 84101 141 X £4.99

Also from BRF

Fired up... not burnt out

Effective children's leadership for today's church
Margaret Withers

Most churches are committed to providing a biblically-based nurture programme for their children, but many rely on the goodwill of parents and other adults to supply the leaders and helpers.

This book is designed to help the non-specialist understand the biblical rationale for nurturing children in the Church and gain the basic skills needed to be an effective leader or helper. Its five sections give a clear and comprehensive guide to the privilege bestowed upon those who work with children. The material covers:

- The importance of children's work and understanding the learning process
- Using signs and symbols and involving children in prayer and worship
- Spiritual development and growing in faith
- Making the Bible accessible
- Enhancing our storytelling and other practical skills
- The wider community and management, health and safety issues

Each section includes introductory notes, Bible readings, thinking and discussion pointers, case studies, practical activities, checklists and short prayers. All the material has been thoroughly field-tested, both with groups and individual readers.

ISBN 1 84101 209 2   £5.99

Also from BRF

Stories, stories everywhere

Good practice for storytellers
Sandra Pollerman

Storytelling is a good thing to do. The experience deepens understanding and encourages hope for the future. As we encounter the stories of our Christian tradition, we are all invited to enter God's story as both story-listeners and story-tellers. From time to time we can help each other to become more effective.

Stories, stories everywhere is a collection of exercises, tips and techniques developed and adapted through experience. It is written for the individual with suggested applications for use with groups. While each chapter can be used on its own, together the ten chapters follow a pattern of development appropriate for storytellers with different levels of experience.

This book will be particularly helpful for those who work in the context of education, worship, spirituality and faith development. It will provide a useful resource, whether we choose to tell our own experiences, retell traditional stories, or stories from the Bible.

ISBN 1 84101 142 8   £6.99

ORDER FORM

REF	TITLE	PRICE	QTY	TOTAL
141 X	*More stories to make you think*	£4.99		
209 2	*Fired up... not burnt out*	£5.99		
142 8	*Stories, stories everywhere*	£6.99		

POSTAGE & PACKING CHARGES		Postage and packing:	
Order value	**UK**		
£7.00 & under	£1.25	Donation:	
£7.01–£30.00	£2.50		
Over £30.00	free	**Total enclosed:**	

Name _____ Account Number _____

Address _____

_____ Postcode _____

Telephone Number _____ Email _____

Payment by: Cheque ❏ Mastercard ❏ Visa ❏ Postal Order ❏ Switch ❏

Credit card no. ❏❏❏❏ ❏❏❏❏ ❏❏❏❏ ❏❏❏❏   Expires ❏❏ ❏❏

Switch card no. ❏❏❏❏❏❏❏❏❏❏❏❏❏❏❏❏❏❏

Issue no. of Switch card ❏❏❏❏   Expires ❏❏ ❏❏

Signature _____ Date _____

All orders must be accompanied by the appropriate payment.

Please send your completed order form to:
BRF, First Floor, Elsfield Hall, 15–17 Elsfield Way, Oxford OX2 8FG
Tel. 01865 319700 / Fax. 01865 319701 Email: enquiries@brf.org.uk

Available from your local Christian bookshop.   BRF is a Registered Charity

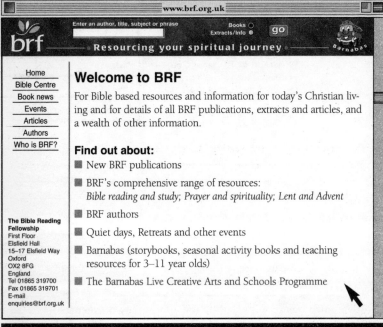

www.brf.org.uk

Enter an author, title, subject or phrase
Books ○
Extracts/Info ●
go

brf — Resourcing your spiritual journey

Barnabas

Home
Bible Centre
Book news
Events
Articles
Authors
Who is BRF?

The Bible Reading Fellowship
First Floor
Elsfield Hall
15–17 Elsfield Way
Oxford
OX2 8FG
England
Tel 01865 319700
Fax 01865 319701
E-mail
enquiries@brf.org.uk

Welcome to BRF

For Bible based resources and information for today's Christian living and for details of all BRF publications, extracts and articles, and a wealth of other information.

Find out about:

- New BRF publications

- BRF's comprehensive range of resources:
  Bible reading and study; Prayer and spirituality; Lent and Advent

- BRF authors

- Quiet days, Retreats and other events

- Barnabas (storybooks, seasonal activity books and teaching resources for 3–11 year olds)

- The Barnabas Live Creative Arts and Schools Programme

Visit the BRF website at www.brf.org.uk

BRF is a Registered Charity